# PARAGRAPH 3

Conversations About *Prepared Leadership* in the Age
of Perpetual Uncertainty–From the C-Suite to the Battlefield

L. KEVIN **KELLY**

LT. GENERAL JOHN **F. MULHOLLAND**
US ARMY (RET.)

KEVIN **MCDERMOTT**

PAGE PUBLISHING, INC.
Conneaut Lake, PA

First originally published by Page Publishing 2021

ISBN 978-1-6624-4456-2 (pbk)
ISBN 978-1-6624-4457-9 (digital)

Printed in the United States of America

*If we want to be good ancestors we should show future generations how we coped with an age of great change and great crises.*

—Jonas Salk, 1967

This book is dedicated with respect to the men and women of the United States Armed Forces, whose reputation for strength and honor in a crisis is unmatched.

# Contents

# Paragraph 3

## Prepared Leadership in the Age of Perpetual Uncertainty

What you are reading is not another how-to leadership book. This is a book about making hard choices when uncertainty and volatility are the core condition of your operating environment. Because that is the condition likely to characterize every environment in the twenty-first century. The upheavals of 2020 were only a first taste.

This is a book about Paragraph 3.

Most military organizations have in common a basic operations order, a structured way of thinking through a challenging mission. The first frames the situation: weather, geography, and the nature of the threat. The second is the mission statement—the who, what, when, where, why for an operation. The *how* is in Paragraph 3. That's the paragraph that is all about execution.

For instance, in 2001 John Mulholland was a colonel commanding the US Army's 5th Special Forces Group (Airborne). In September of that year, just weeks after the 9/11 attacks on the United States, John was given command of Combined Joint Special Operations Task Force-North, code-named Task Force Dagger. The 5th Special Forces Group would be among the very first American combat forces to venture into Afghanistan.

John's mission statement was, to put it mildly, audacious: destroy the Taliban regime and render Afghanistan unsafe for al-Qaeda as a sanctuary. The *how* for doing that—Paragraph 3 of his operations order—was thin, all but blank.

The reason for this was that in September 2001 the United States was in a new place—literally and metaphorically. The senior headquarters to which the 5th SFG(A) was reporting knew virtually nothing about what the Special Forces teams it was sending into Afghanistan would be facing. Hard facts were in short supply. And yet then Colonel Mulholland and his leadership team at Task Force Dagger were expected to make decisions that would affect not just the success of its mission but the survival of those entrusted to carry it out.

On its departure from Fort Campbell, Kentucky, the 5th SFG(A) departed for Karshi-Khanabad, Uzbekistan (K2 for short). This would be Mulholland's first headquarters. As Task Force Dagger made its way into Central Asia John was all too aware of the paucity of intelligence and insight about the ground situation in Afghanistan. As the 5th SFG(A) began setting up its operational headquarters in tents amid the mud of a former Soviet-era airbase at K2, the 5th SFG(A) worked feverishly with comrades from the US Central Intelligence Agency to prepare the initial Special Forces Operational Detachments A (ODAs) for their missions. They were to contact surviving Afghan ethnic militias still fighting the Taliban even though these militias were essentially on their last gasps of meaningful resistance.

After an initial infiltration of an advanced force on the night of October 16, the first two ODAs infiltrated into Afghanistan on the evening of October 19 on MH-47 Chinooks flown by Army special operations aviators of the 160th Special Operations Aviation Regiment. The Nightstalkers, as they are known.

Following these infiltrations, the task force was plagued by some of the worst operational weather ever encountered. Sandstorms and violent weather reaching upward of fifty thousand feet across the mountains of the Hindu Kush made any kind of flying extremely dangerous. Meanwhile Washington was sending pressure from senior headquarters and civilian leadership to get boots on the ground.

Night after night, the task force attempted to infiltrate additional ODAs into Afghanistan. Night after night it was forced back by weather. Pressure from above grew relentlessly to accept extraordinary risk to either fly missions or infiltrate Special Forces teams by other means, such as parachute. Both alternatives posed unacceptable risk to both aircrew and Special Forces soldiers.

There was no playbook for John and his team to call upon. No one with comparable experiences to ask for advice. There was only a lifetime of professional experiences among the task force command. Ingrained appreciation for the fundamentals of war fighting shaped and sharpened their instincts, informing their decision-making. They were a prepared leadership.

By the end of December the mission was accomplished.

For John, Afghanistan was the ultimate test of his preparation as a leader. He went from trying to figure out how to ready the 5th SFG(A) to accomplish anticipated operational requirements to a completely unanticipated war in one of the most challenging operational environments history offers.

We saw a parallel to John's experience in the situation other kinds of leaders confronted in the pandemic of 2020 and in the dramatic social upheavals that accompanied it. Like John, they faced a test of prepared leadership. Like John, they were called upon to fill in a nearly blank Paragraph 3.

In 2020, every kind of organization found itself with an audacious mission statement: Get the world back to work. Make it better than it was. Do it notwithstanding a worldwide health emergency and social unrest the like of which we had not seen for half a century.

Something else we noticed was that many leaders, some of them our colleagues and clients, appeared to be caught unprepared for confronting multiple threats at once. These cascading threats interacted and made their operating environment an ever-more tangled thicket of problems. Some seemed paralyzed by their uncertainty. In military terms they "could not get off the $x$" and act.

In 2020 too many leaders seemed paralyzed in their decision-making, beginning with our political leaders. Leaders who could not get moving did not interest us. They offered no positive lessons. We were interested in leaders with clear ideas about not just surviving the crises that burned hot all through 2020 but capitalizing on them.

So that is who we talked to.

For our purposes the multiple emergencies of 2020 created an ideal moment to discover what distinguished prepared leaders in moments of real crisis. We wanted to capture the thinking of these leaders while the problems they confronted were still live and still raw and before the present had become the past. As we joked among ourselves, it was in some ways like talking to people while their house was still on fire.

You will notice that all our interviewees in *Paragraph 3* are American. That was deliberate. In 2020 the United States found itself in an unaccustomed place. A country that had always assumed its superior capacity to deal with large problems instead found itself flailing in its response not only to the health threat posed by the coronavirus but to the economic calamity and the social unrest that accompanied it. In its prolonged naked unease this was unique in our experience.

In years to come we will begin to forget what life felt like in the long months of 2020, beginning in late winter when the United States shut down almost totally in the space of just two weeks or so in the month of March. Already histories of that moment use March 11 as the symbolic beginning of the crisis. That was the day the World Health Organization officially declared a pandemic. President Donald Trump banned travel from Europe to the United States. The National Basketball Association suspended its season. And the movie star Tom Hanks announced that he and his wife Rita Wilson were both sick with COVID in Australia. They could not come home.

The novel coronavirus had been looming elsewhere since before the start of the year. Now seemingly overnight it had everyone's attention. Within days people were talking about the shutdown. A sense of urgency seized the United States. By the end of March, more than 1,200 cases of coronavirus had been reported.

On March 11, 2021, precisely one year later, there were 62,689 new cases of COVID in the United States. The number of dead since the virus was declared a pandemic was 530,351; the worldwide total was nearly 3 million and rising.[1] Into the spring, more than 50,000 new cases were still being reported across the U.S. every day.[2]

The acceleration of change left us stunned. Even as epidemiologists struggled to understand the nature of the coronavirus medical professionals were being overwhelmed by a flood of COVID patients in hospitals—first on the West Coast, then in the Northeast, and eventually across the whole country. By the end of April 1 million cases of COVID in the United States had been diagnosed. Sixty-three thousand people were dead.

By spring of 2020 anyone who was not an "essential worker"—the instant euphemism for anyone who could not work remotely—was trying to work from their homes or, if they could, from some other place they hoped was safer. Education went online overnight. Schools were asked to transform themselves to deliver distance instruction. The economic and health burden fell heaviest on parts of the United States that were already struggling, especially in Black and Brown neighborhoods.[3]

Then on May 25 George Floyd, a Black man in Minneapolis, was murdered by a police officer, a killing captured in horrible detail by multiple cameras. Protests, sometimes violent, erupted across the country—and not just in the big cities.

It was a sobering, confidence-shaking time for America. The country felt strange to itself. By midsummer, when we began doing our research for this book, so much of what we took for granted about America's economic and social environment seemed to have gone to pieces. A presidential election was brewing for November, and it promised—and subsequently delivered—months of vitriol and acrimony.

---

[1]  "Coronavirus in the U.S.: Latest Map and Case Count." *The New York Times.* March 11, 2021.

[2]  "A pandemic year: Sorrow and stamina, defiance and despair. It's been a year." *The Washington Post.* March 11, 2021.

[3]  See, for example, "COVID-19 Racial and Ethnic Health Disparities." Centers for Disease Control and Prevention. December 10, 2020. See also "State COVID-19 Data and Policy Actions." Kaiser Family Foundation. January 05, 2021.

What was missing was a conversation about a better, revitalized America, ready for the twenty-first century. We had the idea of providing such a conversation in *Paragraph 3*.

Winston Churchill once remarked that in everyone's life there will come a moment when they will be given a chance to do something special, unique to them and suited to their talents. "What a tragedy," Churchill said, "if that moment finds them unprepared or unqualified for that which could have been their finest hour."

Churchill was talking about prepared leadership.

Two things can be said about the preparation of America's leaders in 2020. The first is that in the face of the year's tectonic social upheavals there was a nearly complete absence of commanding ideas from Washington. The second was that leaders from unexpected corners emerged to fill the gaps—business leaders, career military, local police chiefs, medical professionals of every description. Bad as things were in 2020, and they were awfully bad, good leaders were keeping their eye on their missions and on their tomorrows.

The power of these individual stories is the human dimension they bring to the experience of a set of cascading crises so enormous that in 2020 our minds could not process them all at once.

We deliberately did our research at the peak of the multiple crises that erupted throughout 2020. We wanted to capture the perspectives of our interviewees at exactly the moment when the crises were still vivid and the future still unknown. In that sense this book is an oral history of what it felt like to be alive in 2020. We were asking our interviewees to fill in their Paragraph 3 in real time.

In the absence of familiar paths, the leaders we spoke with were drawing on their preparation to make good choices all while everything else seemed to be going to hell.

You will notice that about half our interviewees have spent their entire careers in the private sector. The other half are senior military leaders now thriving in the corporate world, people trained to assume uncertainty and volatility and still see their mission through. Together our interviewees make a wide cross section of race and gender and careers.

We did not ask our interviewees for predictions of the future. Anyone can make predictions, and in 2020 people made a lot of them. But if one looks at the big events in any organization's history, what will strike you is how often transformative events came from beyond the known operating environment. They were events that could not be controlled nor, probably, predicted. And yet they changed the fate of the organization, often abruptly.

We can't know the future. The further out in time we go the less likely we are to be right in our predictions. That is especially true given the volatility and uncertainty that is likely to be with us for a generation. Planning horizons are much nearer than they were even several years ago. Much more useful than predictions is preparing ourselves to assume, oxymoronically, that volatility will be a constant and to prepare our minds for that.

Instead of predictions from our interviewees, we wanted an understanding of what it means to be a prepared leader in the twenty-first century, a century in which volatility and ambiguity will characterize every life.

Our theaters of operation, to use a military term, will be driven by what might be called recombinant risks, a phenomenon that was certainly characteristic of 2020. Recombinant risks are created by the interaction of multiple forces that are not always viewed in combination with one another, producing something novel in our experience. These multiple forces might include not just novel viruses but climate change, demographic shifts, stresses on the global financial system, disruptive technologies and ever more sophisticated cyberthreats. Don't even get us started on politics. In combination these forces create new unforeseen risks—*and* opportunities.

Predictions made in the swirl of crisis tend to have in common that they proceed largely from the forecaster's personal sense of emergency. They are extrapolations of a very compressed period. They assume the future is as inevitable as the sequence of falling dominoes.

Lesson 1 of the interviews in *Paragraph 3*: No future is inevitable. Here is what else we learned.

## Prepared leaders earn the right to lead

In February of 1942, probably the lowest point of World War II for the United States, Franklin D. Roosevelt said bluntly that "the news is going to get worse and worse before it gets better and better, and the American people deserve to have it straight from the shoulder."

It is easy to picture FDR's speechwriters arguing for something a lot more cheerful than that bluntness. But Roosevelt knew he was going to need the trust of the people he led for the long haul. And in the long haul happy talk would only hurt his chances, not help.

Every leader knows there will be days when they need to ask people to do hard things. That becomes next to impossible when there is no trust already in the bank to draw upon. It is much too hard for a leader to start building trust when the world is in crisis. In the winter of 2020 Americans had, in a very grim sense, a fatal lack of trust in what their national leadership was saying about a pandemic that was rapidly transforming not just the United States but the whole world.

With George Floyd's murder in May of 2020 social unrest became an overlapping crisis with the pandemic that continued through the year and across the United States.

At past moments in our history when we faced existential crises leaders arose, somehow, who could appeal to our best instincts as a nation. They stimulated our willingness to make sacrifices for the greater good. But even before coronavirus there was a pervasive—and corrosive—mistrust in leaders that undermined the job of contending with the virus and with its meanings for our futures. This felt like a distinct historical break in the story of the United States.

In June we spoke to Command Sergeant Major Mike Hall, a decorated combat veteran who spent over thirty-four years in special operations. The moment, said Hall, reminded him of certain leadership pronouncements in the early days of the Afghan war.

As Hall remembered, "It was always a response that would make me want to say, 'Listen, you may think this war is going to be over in six months but it isn't. It's going to go on for a long time. We're going to be here for a while.' That's the kind of box we're in now," he said of 2020. "It's a box full of wishful thinking."

In our interviews for *Paragraph 3* the necessity of earning trust—not commanding compliance—came up spontaneously again and again. The military leaders we interviewed, for example, were amused by the idea that in the armed services subordinates can be simply ordered to do a thing and it would happen.

"Even in the military, you might be surprised at how creative soldiers can be at slow-walking your intentions," said Chris Donohoe, the CEO of EX-IQ who spent more than twenty years in Army Special Forces units before retiring as a sergeant major. "If you've built a foundation, if people see you making decisions that have their best interests at heart, then when something pops up that they don't like they are much more willing to give you the benefit of the doubt."

At the center of the military ethos is a commitment to leadership behaviors that bind teams together in mutual loyalty. "In my experience in the private sector," said Donohoe, "I'm not always sure that's part of the ethos of management."

"You want to build trust?" asked retired General Stanley McChrystal, who now heads the McChrystal Group, a strategy and leadership advisory consultancy. "The first thing you do for people is respect them. You're only going to get followership if you build people's desires to follow you. If not, they won't do more than the bare minimum."

Real leaders speak to their teams like adults. As Franklin Roosevelt knew, trust is engendered by an honest communications style. It need not be perfect. If leaders make their direction clear they can improve as they go. If they understand what is needed of them the team will be on board.

"No matter how bad it gets," said J. Michael Prince, "you've got to make sure people trust you. Getting people to follow you is hard when they're afraid and uncertain."

Prince is president and CEO of USPA Global Licensing, the worldwide licensing arm of the US Polo Assn. In the winter of 2020 USPAGL had a matter of weeks to shut down retail outposts, office and supply chains around the world. Central to its success, Prince argued, was the candor of its communications to employees and partners. The objective of this candor was to build a sense of partner-ship not just for the near term but for its post-crisis strategic ambi-tions. Prince and his team recognized early that when a crisis eventu-ally ends organizations will be remembered for how they responded when things were at their worse.

Credible communication is an example of behavior modeling. Modeling the right way of doing things may be the most powerful tool of a prepared leader. Dr. Nadja West, the former surgeon general of the Army who was among the first female graduate of West Point and is now a board member of several large health-care companies, recalled that "in the Army we teach our people what right looks like. If you want to let your soldiers know what the perfect foxhole looks like, dig one and show them how to do it. Now they've seen a cor-rectly constructed foxhole."

Consciously or not, teams take their cues from what leadership does. If leadership is evasive, if leadership is negative, it will infect the ranks.

Trust is engendered, first of all, by an evident commitment to the mission. That is how enduring bonds are built between leaders and their teams. People remember the leaders who put the mission first and their need to be admired second.

At the depths of Britain's fight against fascism Winston Churchill remarked that "people can face any misfortune with forti-tude and buoyancy as long as they are convinced that those in charge of their affairs are not deceiving them or are not dwelling in a fool's paradise."[4] Or, as Mike Hall put it, living in a box full of wishful thinking.

---

[4] Quoted in *Franklin and Winston: An Intimate Portrait of an Epic Friendship*. Jon Meacham. Random House. 2004.

## Sensing change in the environment

The reflex in response to something new is to relate it to something old. The lessons of a past experience—we hope—can be applied to the new problem in front of us. "This is like that," we tell ourselves.

The changes embedded in crisis can be hidden and subtle. The risks in that kind of change—and the opportunities—are not just tactical and immediate. They are long-term. The need for sensing change in the operating environment is self-evident: Misunderstand the nature of a threat and people get hurt. Be blind to opportunity and a crisis goes on longer than it needs to. At such moments experience matters. But experience can also be deluding.

"The way leaders have historically succeeded is by pattern recognition," Orlando Ashford told us. Ashford was president of Holland America Line just at the moment when the coronavirus started its sweep across the planet. "As they progressed up the ladder," Ashford said of the conventional corporate executive, "they've run versions of a specific play for the last twenty-something years. They recognize the patterns and they know what to do. But in today's environment there are patterns we can't recognize."

For example, in the winter of 2020 COVID was sometimes being compared to common influenza. The flu was what we knew and, reassuringly, what we knew how to treat. It took time to realize that COVID, and the social and political crises that subsequently compounded the health crisis, was like nothing we had encountered. The lessons of past experiences were in some cases misapplied.

"Too much of the time we want to believe one situation is similar to another when it's not," said General David M. "Rod" Rodriguez. "We want things to be simple when *none* of it is simple."

In 2014 Rodriguez was assigned to lead nearly three thousand troops in West Africa in combating the Ebola virus, working side by side with Dr. Anthony Fauci, then as now director of the National Institute of Allergy and Infectious Diseases. Part of what Rodriguez learned from the Ebola experience was that "sometimes in managing risks there's a temptation to over-categorize things, to put things in boxes where they don't necessarily fit. Do that and you might miss a huge part of the differences between Ebola and COVID-19 and the responses you need for each."

In a crisis acting reflexively can be fatal to good decision-making. But getting it right is how innovation can happen.

"In some ways," says Larry Drake, a senior partner at Saurus Partners LLC and former president and CEO of Coca-Cola's West Africa division, "you can train your mind for an alertness that tells you 'this moment is different, this is not like that.'"

By the late spring of 2020 it was becoming clear to everyone that the operating environment had changed and changed for everyone. What was not clear was its meaning for the mission—for individual organizations and the country as a whole.

Decision-making based on properly interpreting change in the operating environment could be called the central job of military officers. In preparation for that role they are trained to be conscious of what Orlando Ashford called a sense of situation. A sense, in other words, that the world is moving, or already has moved, someplace new.

Former Admiral William McRaven led Operation Neptune Spear, the successful hunt for Osama bin Laden, and was later chancellor of the University of Texas. "When 9/11 happened," McRaven recalled, "I'd been a member of the special-operations community for 26, 27 years. There was little I had not seen. But the environments that inform your instincts change," he pointed out. "You have to balance instinct with a process."

As difficult as it can be to interpret the present an even more challenging prospect is acknowledging the assumptions we make—consciously or unconsciously—about the future. Prepared leaders cultivate the self-awareness to know that.

Mary A. Legere, for instance, was the Army's foremost intelligence officer when she retired as a lieutenant general. Today she is the managing director for national and defense intelligence at Accenture Federal Services. In an intelligence organization, Legere points out, "We are often reminded that the future, like the enemy, has a vote. That informed the way we rehearsed risks, opportunities and worst-case eventualities that might disrupt a plan."

This idea of rehearsing risks, of *battle drills*, came up repeatedly in our conversations about prepared leadership in advance of crisis. In our exchanges with Legere, for example, she pointed out that prepared leaders are perpetually scanning the future, constantly paying attention to trends in their operating environment. Because there is no other choice. That is a basic requirement of successful risk management.

## Prepared leaders are risk managers

The pandemic of 2020 was a historic failure of risk management. It should not be surprising that among the outstanding leaders with whom we spoke risk management came up in every single conversation.

Though the stakes are radically different, the acceptance of risk is central to the job of leaders in both the military and the corporate worlds. As Steve Beard, CEO of Adtalem Global Education, remarked to us, "Intelligent risk-taking is how you create value. That's what a business is. Even in the context of crisis you're innovating to manage a particular risk. Your innovation may have applications to the way you run a better business on a go-forward basis."

Sometimes an obstacle to smart risk management can be what another one of our interviewees, venture capitalist Neville Teagarden, called "hero culture."

Hero culture is something Teagarden has specifically observed in startup organizations, which may grow up around a talented hero who often turns out to be reluctant to let go of their kingly role as the company matures and the operating environment changes. The consequences are deleterious to any rigorous approach to risk management and certainly to the development of a pipeline of new talent. In military terms, heroes may ironically be a threat to the mission.

The flip side of hero culture is the leader who hands off risk-management accountability to ill-equipped subordinates under the guise of delegation. The perniciousness of shrugging off accountability is exactly that it snowballs down through the organization, all too often to someone not equipped to absorb it, someone with less experience and fewer resources than the boss.

Certainly there are times when a situation warrants delegating extraordinary accountability for risk. And there are times when senior leadership must own all the decision-making. Knowing the difference is derived from accountability to the success of the mission, nothing else.

When John Mulholland was in Afghanistan, for example, his abiding concern was his ability to come to the rescue of his teams if they found themselves in a bad spot. In a crisis his resources would be stretched thin. In some situations the time required to deliver help was nine hours. It was therefore essential for John to give his people, first, an understanding of potential risks. And, second, to provide a clear idea of which risks were theirs to take and which needed to be escalated up the chain of command if they sensed the environment changing.

An example of declining responsibility for risk management at the top might be the posture that the U.S. federal government took with states and municipalities in the spring of 2020 when the national leadership took a backseat in managing the accelerating crisis. The rationale for doing so was delegation to local decision makers. The consequence was horrible for the nation as a whole.[5] It was hard to resist the conclusion that senior leadership was unwilling to be accountable when something eventually went wrong.

Several of our interviewees remarked at this sidestepping of accountability at the top. To put it charitably they found it puzzling. As Kevin McDermott observes, in scenario-planning work pandemics are commonplace and have been for at least the last two decades. A phenomenon like the coronavirus is always on the radar of strategic planners. Or it should be.

"We had a plan for a pandemic," said Dr. Henry Friedman, chief of Medical Neuro-Oncology in The Preston Robert Tisch Brain Tumor Center at Duke University. Friedman was referring to the play-

---

[5] "The End of the Imperial Presidency." Peter Nicholas and Kathy Gilsinan. *The Atlantic.* May 2, 2020.

book for pandemics prepared by the White House National Security Council in 2016.[6] "That was our Paragraph 3," said Friedman. "We *chose* not to execute. In the moment we were paralyzed, waiting for more information."

We all know how attuned organizations are to lapses of character from leadership, no matter how much we hear platitudes about encouraging risk takers. Organizations with weak risk-management regimes are likely to be the same kinds of places where failure is punished. Especially in a crisis, fear of failure's consequences retards the ability to act immediately before too much time passes. In a crisis time is the enemy.

There are better ways to develop the next generation of leaders than by giving them the experience of learning from mistakes. For the prepared leader, the better way is risk guidance—that is to say, elaborating the nature of our risks and working through how they might manifest in the operating environment.

Larry Drake is, like others interviewed for this book, a believer in "battle drills" as a tool of risk management. The idea of a battle drill is to get a team thinking through a range of things that might happen and to be resilient no matter what, especially in the worst case. That is not predicting the future. That is building flexibility to respond to what the future actually delivers. Otherwise the risk in a crisis is to react with analogies to past experience when the problem before us is wholly new.

Leaders are like anyone else in their susceptibility to believing they have their futures all worked out. The feeling of commanding the future because we have thought it all through can be seductive—a seductiveness that will nearly always betray us, as too many of us found out in the winter of 2020.

---

[6] See, for example, "Playbook for Early Response to High-Consequence Emerging Infectious Disease Threats and Biological Incidents." The document was developed by the White House National Security Council in 2016 as a step-by-step guide to managing the risks of pandemics. See also, "Trump team failed to follow NSC's pandemic playbook." Dan Diamond and Nahal Toosi. *Politico*. March 25, 2020.

As Mary Legere put it, "In any age transformational leaders accept the inevitability of volatility. It's possible that COVID may be the catalyst for leaders to think about their relationship to uncertainty. They may learn to think beyond the tyranny of the present."

It is a peculiar thing about risk management that success may go unacknowledged. People are seldom celebrated for the catastrophes that did not happen. Just the same strong leaders shoulder the burden of risk. They don't give it away under the guise of collaboration or delegation. They manage risk no matter how it plays out in a changeable world. This is what several of our interviews called "a moral courage thing."

## Defining courage and confidence in a prepared leader

It would be understandable to presume that the most valuable currency in the military is physical courage. In talking to ex-military leaders for this book what came through strongly was their admiration for moral courage, a character trait that, by example, earns respect from teams that endures as a leader's legacy.

Certainly most of us are not called upon to demonstrate physical courage on a typical day. But in 2020 leaders had to make choices that revealed the content of their character almost daily. Character under pressure is a good definition of moral courage.

It was clear from our conversations that moral courage becomes more fundamental to a leader's success the more senior they become. Senior leaders, after all, are the ones making decisions no one else can make. Frequently that entails enormous individual consequences for members of the team. For the leader the consequence could be reputational risk and career risk. Or the failure of the mission.

We recognize moral courage by its absence. All of us have stories of working for someone who failed to show it: a boss who put their own interests ahead of the mission, who broke trust with the team, who let their personal insecurities guide their decision-making—failures, in other words, of character under pressure.

Twenty-twenty provided countless opportunities to observe character under pressure. Politicians who evaded confrontation and spoke in weasel words. Neighbors who hoarded groceries and found face masks a personal inconvenience. Among the most shocking failures of character under pressure happened on May 25 in Minneapolis. That was the day George Floyd was killed by a police officer, Derek Chauvin, who knelt on Floyd's neck and ignored his pleas that he could not breathe. Those eight minutes and 46 seconds were captured all too vividly on bystander cellphones. A country already tense with the effort of fighting coronavirus erupted in anger at a failure of character, of the absence of moral courage.

We could not help contrasting the killing of George Floyd with so many of the stories told to us by our interviewees. Larry Drake, for instance, remembered being awakened in the middle of the night to be told that a hundred of his employees had been kidnapped and were being held for ransom. Orlando Ashford gave a hair-raising account of trying to bring cruise ship passengers home in the winter of 2020 when ports from Asia to Florida were refusing to let them dock for fear of spreading coronavirus. Mary Legere told of trying to balance the physical well-being of her team at Accenture while at the same fulfilling the national security mission for which her firm had been hired by its clients.

Sometimes with enough distance these stories were told with gallows humor, though far from always. Some moments are just too hard to laugh about. But ultimately all these stories revealed something about the character of the teller. The more senior we are, it seems, the more important the character dimension of leadership becomes.

The debate about whether character can be taught or whether it is a gift from heaven—an inborn temperament—emerged as a through line of this book.

For 250 years the American military professions have been betting that character can be taught as part of every soldier's education. Among our interviewees many argued that character is a personal quality acquired well before leadership training even begins. Others that it is cultivated by reflection on our lived experience.

Kenard "KG" Gibbs of BET Networks remarked to us that "there are people who wither in the face of pressure and people who rise to it. Until you're in a hard situation you may not know who is who." The difference matters, Gibbs argued, because "in a crisis you don't need to be the smartest person in the room. But you need to be surrounded by smart people."

Clearly Gibbs is not someone attached to hero culture in which the leader's personal agenda dominates and collaboration is treated as an impediment. The leaders we spoke to intended to be both collaborative *and* decisive. Call that courage or call it confidence, teams notice.

There is a point, of course, after which leaders cannot collaborate anymore, when, in fact, collaborating begins to look like buck-passing and evasion. A marker of moral courage is owning the burden of deciding. It can be lonely, especially at the higher elevations of an organization. It can test anyone's confidence.

Confidence—sometimes even counterfeit confidence—as an aspect of a leader's character was a frequent topic in our conversations.

This should not be surprising. When Kevin Kelly was CEO of Heidrick & Struggles he dealt personally with the most senior executives in the world. It was a recurring fascination to him that people viewed in their industries as men and women with every reason for self-confidence so often felt like imposters, their flaws just waiting to be exposed.

"Imposter Syndrome," as it is known, is a surprisingly common phenomenon. The phrase itself was first used by psychologists Pauline R. Clance and Suzanne A. Imes in 1978. It turns out to be quite common for strong leaders to go through periods of uncertainty about their ability to prevail, especially in an unfamiliar environment. Research published in the *International Journal of Behavioral Science* in 2011 concluded that as many as seven out of ten successful people experience some degree of impostor syndrome. Often they model a confidence for their teams they do not really feel, knowing that if leadership is negative or hopeless that will cascade down the organization.

"There are times when you're uncertain," said Stanley McChrystal, "and you have just got to act a part. That can be a first step in getting off the *X*, in overcoming inertia and moving out of your comfort zone. I'm not saying it's easy. But you can't let yourself or your organization be paralyzed by crisis, by uncertainty. You have got to get moving."

Problems arise when we lack the self-awareness to acknowledge our insecurities. Without self-awareness the effect on leadership behaviors can be insidious. Think about every bad boss you ever worked for. Ask yourself whether you think they were confident individuals.

The answer to that question, and its effect on real teams, turned out to be a recurring conversation among the prepared leaders we interviewed.

In a crisis the world speeds up. There is a temptation to speed up with it to demonstrate that we're in charge. It is a measure of confidence to resist the temptation to do something *now* solely for the sake of seeming in command. From a lack of confidence in our ability to handle the utterly new we may start believing that, even in the midst of multiple crises like the kind we saw in 2020, nothing about the way we behave needs to change.

Steve Beard, for instance, remarked at how "a lot of folks get to a place of mastery and become so enamored of what they've mastered that they just hold on. But traveling the arc from expert to manager to leader requires you to drop the things you mastered and open yourself to mastering something different. That takes professional courage."

It is hard to say which is worse: the leader blind to the true nature of a crisis or the leader so lacking in self-awareness and so insecure in their ability that they adopt abuse as their dominant character trait.

It is as true in life as it is in leadership that insecurity generates collateral damage. An insecure leader may use their team as tools for advancing their personal interests and career, or become abusive, all out of a desire to protect their own ego.

Compare that to the crisis leadership shown by the city of Boston in its investigation of the Marathon Bombing of April 2013. The relatively rapid resolution of the bombing offered an ideal case to Leonard J. Marcus and Barry Dorn at Harvard's National

Preparedness Leadership Initiative. (Admiral June Ryan, interviewed elsewhere in this book, is a graduate of the NPLI.) Marcus and Dorn describe the collaboration of multiple city, state and federal agencies as a master instance of "swarm intelligence," the almost spontaneous ability of individuals to collaborate in a crisis in pursuit of a shared mission. The conditions for swarm intelligence to occur, they argue, require a shared sense of mission, respect for the responsibilities of others and subordination of the leader's ego to the mission.[7]

Toxic leadership is not forcefulness. It's fear. John saw it at times in his military career when a leader's lack of care and respect for those for whom they were responsible produced a command climate that was, at best, temporary and did not outlive the leader. People knew that in their leader's eyes they were disposable. Often it was not until a new commander arrived and discovered the dumpster fire they inherited that anyone understood what had been happening all along.

DeMaurice "De" Smith, executive director of the NFL Players Association, contended with similar challenges in his negotiations with team owners over the start of the 2020 football season. Owners, he was convinced, were concerned with the potential for lost revenue and not necessarily with the health of football players. This year's players were disposable because next year would deliver a whole new crop of college players. For Smith, though, "the decision-making process is caring for the people we're responsible for."

There is a difference between toxic and being legitimately demanding. In our conversation with Chris Donohoe, for example, he rattled off a list of CEOs, military commanders, and entrepreneurs who accomplished the seemingly impossible with a hard-driving style. The distinction between that style and toxicity is the degree to which people are persuaded that what a leader does is in support of the mission.

---

[7] "Crisis Meta-Leadership Lessons from the Boston Marathon Bombings Response: The Ingenuity of Swarm Intelligence." Marcus et al. National Preparedness Leadership Initiative. 2014. For a lay application of Marcus and Dorn's ideas to the 2020 pandemic, see "What Should Crisis Leadership Look Like?" Douglas Star. *The New Yorker Magazine*. October 26, 2020.

Nothing else.

When John served with Stanley McChrystal the pace was so intense that members of the command jokingly referred to themselves as passengers on the pain train. Jokes aside, they believed McChrystal was changing the way America fights wars. The leadership's purpose, its ethos of mission first, was felt throughout the organization. And so the team was on board. Which bring us full circle to trust.

*Paragraph 3* is not the history of leadership during the COVID crisis. What we have done instead is describe the constants of prepared leadership in any age but especially in an age like the one we live in now, an age in which what becomes normal are upheavals on a worldwide scale and the short lives of familiar operational assumptions.

The pace of these upheavals will sometimes be stunning in their suddenness, as we saw during the COVID pandemic. If there will be a constant in the twenty-first-century upheaval it will be that.

The job of prepared leaders will be to ready themselves and their organizations on a tactical level, certainly, but especially on a human level. The ideas described in the following pages are a field manual for getting the job right.

# A Painful Epiphany

## Admiral William H. "Bill" McRaven, Retired

*When Bill McRaven was selected as chancellor of the University of Texas system in July of 2014 he was still a month away from leaving the US Navy. Over 37 years, McRaven had risen to four-star admiral, admired for an innovative record as a Navy SEAL.*

*At his retirement, McRaven was commanding the US Special Operations Command. In his previous job as commander of the Joint Special Operations Command, McRaven organized and oversaw Operation Neptune Spear, the special ops raid that led to the killing of Osama bin Laden on May 2, 2011.*

*After the September 11 terrorist attacks McRaven spent almost all his time in counterterrorism work. Terrorism would prove to be a good analogy for the coronavirus that attacked the whole world in 2020. Even with the inadequate information available to the government in the winter of 2020, McRaven believes a rigorous acceptance of the inevitability of contingency would have prevented the worst.*

*Pandemics are a conventional element of scenario planning and not just in the military. With a more disciplined approach to preparing for unforeseen events—even Black Swan events like the coronavirus—McRaven is convinced the United States could have fought "a conventional war, with doctors and researchers and people wearing masks able to confront the enemy as it hit our borders." Instead, by the summer of 2020 we were engaged in a counterinsurgency fight against an ingenious enemy attacking on multiple fronts.*

*It was, says McRaven, a failure of preparation and a failure of risk management—twinned elements he treats as intrinsic to prepared leadership.*

*Prepared leaders rehearse for crisis—battle drills, McRaven calls them. Battle drills can, among other uses, reveal how the operational landscape may have shifted in ways that can be fatal—maybe literally so—when the worst happens. They are a concept borrowed from the military but one that McRaven has seen applied successfully in the civilian world, most particularly in moments of crisis at the University of Texas. Their virtue is in providing a blueprint for action at a moment when events may heighten emotion and cloud vision.*

*"When you're in a crisis," McRaven observes "everything is exaggerated—the consequences of the decisions you make, the urgency you feel. It's not the time to be walking through all your trouble spots."*

*In and out of the military, McRaven has learned from hard experience that, in a crisis, boldness and swagger can be the enemies of smart risk management. In 2020 the rest of us learned that lesson too. Prepared leaders, McRaven argues, know their mission, know their risks, know their jobs and know their organizations. And they rehearse for the worst.*

*In his (virtual) appearance at the Aspen Ideas Festival in the grim summer of 2020 McRaven told the audience he describes himself as an optimist. The United States has faced dark moments and heartbreaking complexity in the past, he pointed out, and risen to the occasion. What those occasions had in common, he observes, was inspiring leadership.*

I'm guessing it was maybe November of 2008. I go to see the US ambassador in Kabul and I'm thinking we're going to drink tea and make official calls. Instead it's just me. He starts telling me the war has been a failure and partly it's because of my guys. He tells me, "You're not communicating with us. You're running your own agenda. You're not coordinated with anybody on the ground. You've done it all your way." Finally I've had enough and we're yelling back and forth. I'm like, "Are you kidding me? I've got guys *dying* on the battlefield. And you're insinuating that the reason we're in the place we're in is because we haven't done a good job?" I was livid.

I got on the helicopter to fly back to Bagram and I started thinking about what the ambassador said. I called the command team together and asked them whether the ambassador could be right. I was still not convinced.

We did a top-to-bottom review of the command. In January the staff came back to me and ran through all sorts of things that needed to change. None of them were on the margin. They were all big turns of the organization. I realized the ambassador was right. It was a painful epiphany that was born out of hard review. The landscape had changed out from under us, and we had not changed with it.

When 9/11 happened I'd been a member of the special-operations community for 26, 27 years. There was little I hadn't seen. But the environments that inform your instincts change. You have to balance instinct with a process. That's one definition of prepared leadership.

With COVID, once we determined that we were in the middle of a crisis instead of pulling together—you know, 50 states with a coordinated effort—we did the opposite. It wasn't because we didn't understand the risk. It was poor leadership. In 2020 we were devoid of leadership.

In the middle of a crisis, obviously, the things you thought about ahead of time haven't unfolded the way you expected. If they had you would have addressed them. If we understood on day one how virulent this virus was then we may have approached it differently.

In the graduate-school class I teach at the University of Texas we ran a pandemic scenario. In the scenario the students are members of the National Security Council and I was the president being briefed. In 2020 the date of the exercise in the scenario was late February. We were running the scenario about mid-March. By then we saw the trend line moving up and the students were, of course, all second guessing. They're saying, "Well, Mr. President, we need to close down businesses." And I'm saying, "Why would we close down businesses? I'm not going to do that." At the end of the conversation we all came to the realization that in February we probably would have made the same decisions as President Trump.

It was a lesson in how to think about risk. If you don't understand your opponent you underestimate the risk.

We mishandled the virus from the get-go. Had we handled it appropriately we'd have been fighting a conventional war, with doctors and researchers and people wearing masks able to confront the enemy as it hit our borders. Instead we allowed the virus to proliferate throughout the population. It became a pandemic insurgency. We were fighting on its terms and on multiple fronts. By the time the enemy got around our Maginot Line we were screwed.

When you're in a crisis everything is exaggerated—the consequences of the decisions you make, the urgency you feel. It's not the time to be walking through all your trouble spots.

In the middle of a crisis you don't want to be thinking on your feet more than you have to. Battle drills are a great analogy here. If it's a SEAL platoon walking down a jungle path in Vietnam getting ambushed you have a battle drill for how to get out of the kill zone. You're reacting to the crisis based on the preparation you'd done before.

In the military the sense of contingency is part and parcel of the culture. In a command position you're always asking yourself, Am I prepared to deal with the next crisis?

Military commanders get a CCIR, or the commander's critical information requirements. It includes a list of ten worst-case scenarios—somebody dies, something bad makes the *Washington Post*, we go to war. You ask yourself if you're prepared to handle each one of those crises. Have you war-gamed them? You not only have to deal with the here and now, which is challenging in itself. You also have to be able to deal with the worst case.

In the corporate world I've found planners are happy to plan a best-case scenario, happy to plan a realistic scenario. But they are reluctant to plan a worst-case scenario. Part of it is they don't want to spook the market. Part of it is they're just kind of hoping they never get to that point. Part of it is they think it's unrealistic, and why spend time working on something unrealistic? But the unforeseen happens more often than not. If you're not planning for the worst case you're probably not a good leader.

What happens if this pandemic goes on for another two years? You might say, well, the trend lines tell us we will start to recover by early next year or we'll get a vaccine. What happens if that doesn't occur? How are you going to save your company?

In the military we always started with the worst case, which is nuclear war—the least likely to happen. Down at the bottom is low-intensity conflict, which has the least impact globally but is the most likely to happen. It's the reason special operations have been so prominent. But you *still* have to prepare for nuclear war.

In any leadership position you should be anticipating as part of your normal processes, doing battle drills for the things that might happen. Because environments change.

When I was at the Naval Postgraduate School I did my thesis on the theory of operations. I found those that were successful were not the ones where guys had incredible bravado and accepted high risk. Instead, they took as much of the risk out of operations as they could by hiring the right people and doing the planning, doing the rehearsal.

Early in my Navy career my first assignment was the underwater demolition team. We were being trained by Vietnam vets who said, "Here's the five-paragraph platoon leader's order. That's all you need to know." Well, the complexity of an underwater mission was such that you had to plan each phase of the mission in great detail. By planning and rehearsing you could reduce risk to a manageable level. But I was criticized by the commanding officer for not being *special* enough for special operations. Those guys wouldn't understand why they couldn't do complex missions based on a PLO.

When I came in as a new officer and took over one of the teams I said we were going to do some hard planning. They didn't want to at first, but then we started doing rehearsals and, surprise, we got better. It becomes so instilled that folks who manage a particular part of a portfolio all come together as a piece of the puzzle. The same would be true in business.

The interesting thing about risk and the world of academia is risk *aversion*, an aversion to making hard decisions sometimes. We might have an incident on the campus, for example, and sometimes it was difficult to get the leadership to take decisive action because they were concerned about litigation or political backlash or the media. We constantly worked at shaping their decision process by saying, "Look, here are the risks. Yes, we can be sued. Yes, it may not look good in the pages of the *Austin American-Statesman*. But the other risk is you're not addressing a problem affecting your faculty and your students." If you don't address problems aggressively you're going to get *more* problems.

When I was in the Joint Special Operations Command the command sergeant major came and told me we had a problem with sexual harassment and sexual misconduct. I started talking to the chaplains and I started talking to the doctors. They were appropriately protecting the names of the women. But where I jacked them up was in telling them they had a responsibility to tell me when there were bad things happening at the command line. We turned over all the rocks. We had a problem and we got on it aggressively.

When I got to UT I wanted to do a survey to see whether we had a similar problem. A lot of people said we might not like what we found out. Well, we didn't. Across the university system there was a problem. But it enabled us to address the problem and get out ahead of it. There was a risk, and it was the risk of not acting.

Every time I went to a new command I spent time finding out as much about it as I could. You talk to folks to understand where the shortfalls are, where the strengths are. When I went to run the University of Texas system that was probably the biggest transition I ever had. I immediately called all my staff that were going to be working for me to Washington, DC, and we spent a week or so going through everything. I wanted to understand everyone's role and what they wanted. It was about preparing to lead. The only way to be prepared to do that is to understand the terrain, the human terrain, the mission terrain.

Even when you get to the top job you're never *not* preparing to lead. If you get to the point where you think you have nothing further to learn you've probably lost your passion.

I went out of my way early on to understand the nuances and the details of command, the organization I was coming into. At UT it was, what does the chair of a department do? What does the dean do? How do you get formula funding? Once you understand the culture you're in a position to shape it in a way that is a good mixture of the old and the new.

I was often asked about the transition from the military to academia. In the military, they'd ask, don't you just tell people what to do and they do it? I would tell them you don't just tell soldiers what to do. Soldiers have to be inspired and motivated, just like a faculty. Soldiers expect their leaders to lead, and so do faculty.

Leaders are always a product of the people who surround them. At the University of Texas I had the best staff I ever had in my entire career, military or civilian. It was like having a staff of all generals who were incredibly experienced, incredibly thoughtful, just really good at what they did. What the college presidents did well was look at scenarios. You know, what happens if the price of oil drops and we no longer get the amount of money we need? What happens when we have an active shooter? What happens if a faculty member gets accused of a crime? They dealt with those issues pretty well.

We had a terrible tragedy on the campus. A woman was killed and then in a separate incident a crazy guy stabbed someone and killed them. Two murders within a year. I went over to meet with the college president when one of these events was unfolding, and they were exercising the planning they'd done on just such a tragedy. They called in all the right people. They made all the notifications. They were really good. It gets back to the battle drill. The leadership didn't have to say, "Gee, what do we do next?" They knew what to do.

When you look back at the Iraq invasion there was always a criticism that we didn't have a plan for what happened when we won the fight. But there is always someone in the military doing future planning. Every major staff has got a J3 who is responsible for operations and a J5 who is responsible for fighting the future. The expectation is that somebody's always gonna be looking down the road and saying, "Okay, when we win this fight how will we come out of it stronger? What are our next steps?" Every organization needs an equivalent of a J5.

I would offer that, generally, the long-term plan is optimistic because you've won the current fight. The fight we're in now is going to be a long, hard slog. Nobody should think otherwise. But because of this crisis we're going to learn things. We're going to learn how to make vaccines faster, make therapeutics faster. We're going to learn that leadership at the top matters, that you have to have a federal coordinated response from the White House. That you can't just go willy-nilly to all the various states and counties and cities. Next time we'll be prepared to do better.

With all the social upheaval that's happening we will come out stronger. Invariably as a nation we've risen to the occasion—*when* we have the right leadership.

# A Sense of Situation

## Orlando Ashford

*In years to come, people may forget the abruptness with which the world fell into crisis because of the coronavirus. They would do well to listen to Orlando Ashford's stories of trying to bring home Holland America's cruise ships from the far-flung ports of the world.*

*Whether they had the virus aboard or not, cruise ships in the winter of 2020 were suspected of carrying the infection until it could be proven they didn't. Stories of glamorous ships wandering the seas in search of a port that would accept them became international news. Ashford, as president of Holland America, was in charge of fixing the problem, and quick.*

*The president of a cruise line operates internationally in half a dozen businesses at once: entertainment, travel, restaurants, logistics, hotels. He is also the admiral of a small navy sailing open seas to multiple countries. In Ashford's case, he presided over a fleet of 14 vessels carrying more than 900,000 guests annually to all seven continents.*

*And in the winter of 2020 it all stopped at once.*

*Ashford came to Holland America in 2015 from Mercer, the global consulting firm for which he was president of its Talent Business segment. While at Mercer he wrote the book* Talentism, *an examination of the ways technology and human networks may bridge skills gaps and improve business performance. Previously Ashford had been chief human-resources and communications officer at Mercer's parent company, Marsh & McLennan Companies. Earlier, he held a progressively more senior string of roles at Coca-Cola, Motorola, Ameritech and Andersen Consulting.*

*Today Ashford is the executive chairman of Azamara, the boutique cruise line. He also serves on the board of directors of ITT, Hershey Entertainment & Resorts Company, Virginia Mason Medical Center and Year Up, a year-long intensive training program for underserved young adults. The way he tells stories of his multiple experiences defines the difference between managing through a crisis and leading through one.*

*In the case of the homeless cruise ships, for example, Ashford recognized that the chaos caused by coronavirus was different from other crises he'd experienced.*

*"There was so much I didn't know going in," Ashford says now, "and that I had about three minutes to figure out. That was the type of pressure we were under." He jokes that "there's no class in B school that prepares you for these things."*

*The coronavirus was different—and not just in its fully international scope. That made its problems different. But there were specific leadership philosophies that Ashford had acquired in his past that, in the midst of crisis, he drew upon consciously.*

*With both his organization and his customers, for example, he was transparent in his communications even when the news wasn't what anyone wanted to hear. And he relied on the collective intelligence of his organization, a trait he contends will be essential in navigating the kinds of unforeseeable crises likely to define the twenty-first century.*

*"You need to draw on experiences that may seem completely unrelated to what you're dealing with," Ashford argues. "You need to pull from those experiences, learn from those around you, and make the most informed decision you can."*

*Prepared leaders, he says, will need to fight the impulse to approach a novel event as if it were a variant of every crisis they ever fought before.*

*"The way leaders have historically succeeded is by pattern recognition," he points out. "As they progressed up the ladder they've run versions of a specific play for the last twenty-something years. They recognize the patterns and they know what to do. But in today's environment there are patterns we can't recognize."*

*The winners, he believes, will have what he calls a sense of situation, a sense of where the world is going.*

In 2016 we were in Istanbul when there was an attempted coup against the government. If we pulled our cruises out of that port there was going to be a financial impact because Turkey was a high-revenue destination. It still is. Pull Istanbul out of a cruise and the value of the cruise drops significantly—probably 30-plus percent. Your impulse is to try and squeeze in as many more cruises as you can. But reading the tea leaves I could see there was a risk of death and civil unrest in that part of the world. If we had an incident on board a ship the devastation to our business would be significant. You weigh that against the short-term loss—the incremental value of another cruise, in other words, versus the long-term protection of your business. We pulled out.

That was a useful experience to have had in the winter of 2020. But it was not exactly the same as the pandemic.

For three months of 2020 I was trying to negotiate with countries to get my ships accepted into a port, trying to negotiate with embassies and government agencies, trying to get my guests onto chartered flights and get them safely home. There was so much I didn't know going in and that I had about three minutes to figure out. That was the type of pressure we were under.

I was in the cruise industry for about five-and-a-half years at that point. Most of the people around me were veterans for twenty or thirty years, which is how it is in the cruise business. There were people who said, "It's okay, we've done this before with SARS. Don't overreact. We're fine."

There was a Princess ship that was in Japan with COVID cases on it. And we had a ship, the *Westerdam*, that was suspected of having COVID on it just because it was a ship and in Asia. Turned out there were no cases on the *Westerdam* but we needed to prove that.

Meanwhile it was being denied entry in all the different ports of Asia. My ship floated in that region for eight days.

Multiple times a day we were in contact with the captain of the *Westerdam* as we tried to find a place for her to dock. We'd tell him, "Here's what we're working on at corporate with local governments." We'd ask, "What's going on? What do you need? How are things going on with the crew?" Ultimately we got the *Westerdam* into Cambodia and got all those folks off the ship.

We became a political football. There were no direct flights from Phnom Penh to some of the major cities we needed to go through. We ended up connecting through Malaysia and Singapore. And the next thing we know, Malaysia has grabbed one of our guests off her plane to test her and she has COVID. So everything shuts down.

The whole time I'm stuck sitting in my emergency resource center in Seattle. Finally I stood up and said I need four or five volunteers to go to Cambodia so we can figure this out. Within five hours we were on our way. We didn't know if we were going for three days, three weeks or three months. But we had to get better information and work toward a solution.

Try to imagine 600 people in the lobby of a hotel in Phnom Penh. You had representatives from different countries and embassies. Everyone's screaming and all kinds of craziness. Some people are freaked out. Nobody can go anywhere.

First thing I did was, I told everyone, "Stop." We got the hotel's theater cleared out. We brought all 600 people into this space and I addressed them. I told them we were going to have meetings in that room every day at ten in the morning and two in the afternoon. And I would tell them what was going on. I stayed there and answered every question, whether they were nice or whether they were over the top. We went through that until we had answers and got everybody on planes and got them home.

About a month later we had a situation with a ship in Florida. First we had to navigate through the Panama Canal. We had a few COVID cases on the ship. We sent another healthy ship to the aid of the first one. It had no guests on her, just crew. We wanted to send that second ship to try to lighten the passenger load on the first, add extra doctors, provide help. But while it was en route members of the crew, out of fear, started to wind themselves up. They did not want to help the other ship and were going to refuse to come out of their rooms.

I got the call in Seattle. We talked to the captain and we talked to the officer team. The suggestion was that I needed to motivate the troops. My normal MO would have been to get on a plane and fly down to the ship, to lead from the front. But I *couldn't* fly because of COVID. I had to do this via conference call.

I talked to all 700 crew in the ship's theater on its speaker setup. I answered every single question for almost three hours. I said, "There'll be no punishment for anyone who refuses to work." But I bet on their seafarer spirit that enough of them would volunteer to help because if the circumstances were reversed they'd want somebody to come help them. And that's what happened.

There's no class in B school that prepares you for these things.

The way leaders have historically succeeded is by pattern recognition. As they progressed up the ladder they've run versions of a specific play for the last twenty-something years. They might run bigger and more complex versions of the play but it's essentially the same play. They recognize the patterns and they know what to do. But in today's environment there are patterns we can't recognize.

An executive who has been in a system a long time, who knows everything about everybody's job and can dictate to everybody from where they sit at the top—that's an inefficient and dangerous leadership model. Things change too quickly. If I felt that way before COVID I really feel that way now.

In order to be prepared you need to be ready to draw on experiences that may seem completely unrelated to what you're dealing with right now. You need to pull from those experiences, learn from those around you, and make the most informed decision you can. It's a combination of having people around you who you can tap into for information and then being able to quickly collate all that and make decisions.

When people talk to me about my concept of leadership I always respond by talking about collective intelligence. A group outperforms an individual. And a diverse group outperforms a homogeneous group. That's how I position myself to have impact.

In order to tap into the collective intelligence you have to listen. You have to synthesize what you're hearing and articulate a point of view. As the leader, you have to say, "This is what we're going to do."

The other concept I believe in is being learning agile, to have a sense of situation. Striking the balance among listening and instructing and communication is critical. Take the input, then make your decision about how to move forward.

I find resistance to new thinking fascinating—especially during COVID. The pace at which business is changing requires more reliance on curiosity. When I think about a world post-COVID I'm convinced that if we're going to work our way out of this people are going to have to depend more on being learning agile and on collective intelligence.

I'm intellectually curious. I'm a smart guy. But there are people who know things I don't. I'm willing to trust expertise that is different from mine. When somebody presents me with something really new I say, "Wow, exciting. Now how do I determine if what you're telling me is true?"

I'll give you an example of what I mean. I spent several months in 2020 exploring different therapeutic options that could help mitigate or even protect against COVID. When I told people I knew of a product they could apply to their face and hands and it would protect them three to five hours per application they were interested. But when I suggested their organizations try it to protect employees they backed up. Their resistance came into play because they didn't understand it. Not that you shouldn't kick the tires on things. But I am sometimes really shocked at the lack of intellectual curiosity I see.

As an individual, my philosophy is to try and be as transparent as possible, especially in a crisis. There are certain things a senior leader can't say, of course. You never want to create fear, and there are issues that might be material that you can't share. But sharing how a situation is playing out—good, bad or indifferent—is a better approach.

You may think you're protecting your employees, protecting the average person by sugarcoating. But if you make happy-talk statements early on in a crisis—"I don't anticipate any job loss" or "We'll all have bonuses next year"—and then later have to back off those statements it impacts your trust. You don't have credibility.

You can't get freaked out by the enormity of a specific situation. The enormity of it determines your sense of urgency and how hard you have to work. But at the end of the day, if you do the smart things, this too shall resolve.

"It will resolve." That's always my answer to a question about how a crisis ends. On the *Westerdam* people couldn't stay aboard forever, they couldn't stay in a hotel forever. It had to resolve. We just had to figure out how. I don't know if it's today or three days from now or three weeks from now. But we'll work and we'll figure it out.

That model of communications works for me. If you're clear on your objectives, if you tap into the people around you, put a strategy in place, a crisis resolves. And more often than not you win.

Some of the stories I've told you have been extreme. But I've been through a lot of situations in my career. At the moment a thing might seem like the biggest project or the biggest initiative or the most important problem. But at some point it ends. They all resolve.

Early in the COVID crisis there were a lot of people saying, "Well, this isn't as bad as we think. Things are going to come back. We'll figure this out." All the while it was steadily getting worse. We had to make decisions and figure out things—be curious—that might help. Take it on as a challenge to your leadership.

I do think there are people who are natural leaders and will have better instincts in extreme situations than others. But leaders at whatever level can be made better through education, wherever they start.

I frame my estimation of leaders in the COVID crisis in terms of being able to make decisions. You have to *move*. To make a non-decision is riskier than making the wrong decision. You can always correct direction and go on.

No one's ever 100 percent. But if you do nothing and just sit, hoping the world's going to come back together, you're creating new problems.

It's hard to predict what will stick with us about the way we were doing things in this crisis. Think, for example, about how we're leading and managing and making decisions without being able to physically touch. People were starting to hire executives completely remotely—the same people who would have told you before COVID they would never hire a CEO or senior person without everyone meeting them live and in person. Executives who said they would never lead a team on which everybody works from home. After COVID they were forced to.

Some people believe you can run the world without ever seeing anybody. And in some scenarios we've seen production increase by using technology platforms. But I don't think we'll ever completely get away from the need to have human interaction. It may happen differently with different frequency. Figuring out that balance will be important for the next generation of leaders.

Leaders who are wired this way will become more important. Right now the world is pivoting around the idea of a vaccine. The world has been disrupted. Some people think the minute we get a vaccine we'll go back to where we were. I don't see a vaccine as a panacea that will get us all back to where we were. The world will have to figure out how to live with COVID, just as after 9/11 we did not travel the same way we used to. Before we can take a flight we take off our shoes and we have to be scanned and assessed in ways that we were not before. That changed forever how we interact with each other. It will be the same with COVID.

Those who are waiting for the magic bullet to bring us back to the way things were are missing a window. They're waiting for the old business model.

You see it in the cruise industry. There are people who grew up in the industry a certain way, and the idea of the world not being like it once was is so disheartening to them that they've decided to wait the virus out. And then there are others who are saying, "Hey, look, there's a huge disruption right now." There are adaptations that will need to happen but this is a huge opportunity.

The second group will be at a competitive advantage. They're the ones who are going to be intellectually curious about what the new world will look like. That will allow them to get to the future world quicker.

The winners have a sense of situation. They figure out where the world is going and make adaptations to take advantage of it. The world will be better off.

# You Just Keep Marching

## Dr. Nadja Y. West, Lieutenant General, US Army (Retired)

*Again and again in* Paragraph 3 *our interviewees have made the case that character is at the center of prepared leadership. Character is the quality that opens the mind and informs smart behaviors. The open question is where character comes from.*

*Nadja West is squarely in the camp of "character is training."*

*"Character is doing the right thing at the right time for the right reason," says West. "In the Army, we teach our people what right looks like. If you want to let your soldiers know what the perfect foxhole looks like," she says, "dig one and show them how to do it. Now they've seen a correctly constructed foxhole."*

*West's career has been a collection of firsts. She was among the first women admitted to West Point and is the highest-ranking woman the academy has produced. In 1988 she earned her MD from George Washington University School of Medicine. Today she serves on the boards of, among other organizations, Johnson & Johnson, Tenet Healthcare, Nucor Corp. and Americares.*

*West deployed during both Operations Desert Shield and Desert Storm during her family-medicine residency at Martin Army Hospital in Fort Benning, Georgia. In 2013 she became the first African American woman to hold the rank of active-duty major general. Two years later, she was promoted to lieutenant general and named the 44th US Army surgeon general and commanding general of the US Army Medical Command—the first African American woman to hold either position.*

*In addition to other accomplishments, West holds the title of Iron Soldier, an honor earned while serving as the Division Surgeon for 1st Armored Division—an assignment she considers among the highlights of her career.*

*For all her achievements, when West talks about the character traits of leadership the first ones she mentions are empathy and humility, even before adaptability and agility. In part West means the willingness to learn from subordinates and colleagues. She also means a willingness to show care for her team.*

*"If you're a senior leader," says West, "of course your subordinates are required to obey your lawful orders. But there is a difference between just ordering people around and providing purpose, direction and motivation. That's the Army's definition of leadership. Let them know that you care about them, that you value them, that they belong to the team."*

*In 2014, when she was the Joint Staff Surgeon, West was part of the team that met early on to devise potential Department of Defense contributions to the US response to the Ebola crisis. The multidisciplinary, multiagency team provided recommendations to the Chairman of the Joint Chiefs of Staff so that he might offer courses of actions to the President for consideration. Preparedness was essential to the success of the Ebola response mission, says West. Crucial to that preparedness was a spirit of inclusiveness demonstrated by the members of the Joint Staff.*

*"An essential part of risk-mitigation planning," West argues, "is being inclusive and asking one another, 'Hey, what do you think?' That vets risks beforehand. You're given the opportunity to listen to the perspectives of other stakeholders." In 2020 West remained deeply convinced that this openness was crucial to the effectiveness of the US response that prevented a horrible viral disease from becoming far worse than it was.*

*Twenty-twenty was a discouraging year. There is no denying it. But West takes consolation from the history of other discouraging years, notably 1918, when the end of the First World War was still a year away and an influenza pandemic ravaged the planet.*

*"We learn in the military," says West, "that you keep going, you just keep marching. You don't surrender to the emotions of the moment."*

You will hear people assert that we are either born knowing the right thing or we're not. I do not agree. You can learn. Character can be cultivated.

When I was a brand-new plebe at West Point I remember once getting a pretty stern talking-to. My roommate had come to formation with the belts of her full-dress gray uniform twisted in the back where she couldn't see it. My squad leader asked me, "Why did you let your roommate go out like that?" It was not a conversation about belts at all. It was teaching me about responsibility for my teammate. It was about leadership. It was about being a servant leader. It was about what it means to be a leader of character.

Leaders are prepared, first, as human beings. They need to be adaptable to changing environments, and they need to be agile in adjusting to the speed of change. They need to be ready for everything and comfortable with uncertainty. And they can't be whiny about it.

The Army provides opportunities to hone these attributes just by the way we serve. Every three or four years we may be reassigned by a process called a permanent-change-of-station move. When you serve all over the US and around the world you learn the culture of those places and you learn resilience. That adaptability helps you be a prepared leader.

There may be a perception that the culture of a regimented military organization is not conducive to expressing empathy.[8] But the phrase "soldiering is an affair of the heart" is attributed to an Army WWII veteran, General Creighton Abrams. You have to love your soldiers. You have to love your team. You have to respect them as people first. To do that you have to get to know them.

To have an organization that's high functioning everybody needs to feel part of it. Everyone needs to feel a sense of belonging. I have worked in organizations where that was not the case. Where sometimes I thought, man, if I'd had this job earlier I probably would not have stuck around. In cases like that you find yourself thinking,

---

[8] "Lt. Gen. Nadja Y. West on the Power of Empathy." Adam Bryant. *The New York Times*. June 30, 2017.

gosh, look at how much more we could do if we weren't burdened with this climate. You learn what right looks like look like, you learn what wrong looks like.

When I was Army Surgeon General we had 135 thousand people—soldiers and civilians—in the Army Medical Department. In my first-day briefing I told my direct subordinates "Don't change my tone" in communicating my orders. Because my tone is deliberately about dignity and respect. I learned that from General Casey in 1st Armored Division. When I showed up in 1999 I was given the nickname Iron Doc. I was not the Female Iron Soldier. I was not the Black Iron Soldier. I was made to feel like a valued member of the team.

If you're a senior leader, of course, your subordinates are required to obey your lawful orders. But there is a difference between just ordering people around and providing purpose, direction and motivation. That is the Army's definition of leadership.

Your teammates are people. They have multiple dimensions to them. Of course, we're not going to hold people's hands and say, "Please could you do this?" They need to get their job done. But let them know you care about them, that you value them, that they belong to the team.

When General David Perkins was Commanding General of the U.S. Army Training and Doctrine Command he conducted a professional-development session for my MEDCOM headquarters team. His approach to leading during uncertain times was to keep in mind not only what a team *does* but what it's ultimately *for*. That will keep you focused during turbulent and rapidly changing conditions. When we don't understand that it's too easy to get buffeted by changing situations and requirements.

A leader does not need to have all the answers. Of course we need to be subject-matter experts in our areas. We need to be competent so that people will be confident in our ability to lead them. But especially in moments of uncertainty and dealing with complex problems we need the contributions of our team with their diverse skillsets, perspectives and potential solutions.

An essential part of risk-mitigation planning is being inclusive and asking one another, "Hey, who do you think?" That way risks are vetted beforehand. You have given yourself the opportunity to listen to the perspectives of other stakeholders.

During the Ebola outbreak in 2014 I served with General David Goldfein, who was director of the Joint Staff at the time. I was on the Joint Staff team and was the Chairman's doc. General Goldfein was a phenomenal leader, extremely inclusive. If someone asked questions he valued that. When I told him I thought we needed to talk to the Chairman of the Joint Chiefs of Staff about Ebola before it was really a big deal he could have easily asked, "How is it militarily relevant?" Instead he took the time to learn about it. That gave him the opportunity to war game well before Ebola was emergent.

General Martin Dempsey, the Chairman, was the same way. He brought together individuals from academic institutions in a kind of summit to ask what we could do about Ebola even before we were asked. When General Dempsey wrote his book[9] he included a chapter on the inclusivity of our Ebola mission. We war-gamed the logistics piece and defined our strengths. That gave us time to look at how we named the risks and mitigated them.

Today I sit on the board of Nucor. One of Nucor's first CEOs was Ken Iverson. Early in his career in 1962 he was sent to South Carolina to run a steel mill there. He went to meet with his team and pointed out that there was a wall between the Colored breakroom and the White breakroom. Iverson said, "We can't have this. I need to work with a team." And they took down the wall.[10]

Given the volatile nature of the metals industry Nucor needs to have a preparedness mindset. It has uptimes and downtimes, construction cycles, lean times, boom times. That's why decades ago Nucor was the first to commit to electric arc furnaces. They are much more agile that way. It's why Nucor is still around while some big

---

[9] Radical Inclusion: What the Post-9/11 World Should Have Taught Us about Leadership. Martin Dempsey and Ori Brafman. Missionaryday. 2018.
[10] Plain Talk. Ken Iverson. Wiley. 1997.

competitors folded. Nucor had a smarter approach to risk management. When you are prepared you can pivot in any situation.

When you are confronted with a novel situation a basic set of principles—a framework—can get you through. Everything may be uncertain but if you have a framework you can name your risks and create controls. We might not have known about COVID, for example, but we knew about infectious diseases. Washing hands, coughing and sneezing responsibly, appropriate social distancing—we knew those things minimized exposure to infectious agents before we completely knew the specifics of transmission, incubation periods and so on. We had a framework to fall back on while we were working out the details.

Risk management has levels, of course. When I was a brand-new intern in Fort Benning in 1988 the whole concept of risk was about making sure I learned my craft as a family-medicine physician. Did I have the required skills? Did I know how to accurately diagnose the patient? If I didn't ask the right questions or didn't order the right test that might lead to an incorrect diagnosis. That level of risk was on my mind continuously. Not that you wanted to be fearful. But as a new doctor you wanted to make sure you respected the gravity of what you were doing. If you were a clinic chief, by contrast, your responsibilities, priorities and risks were different.

General Goldfein used to say risk is a dynamic thing. You should always ask, "Risk for whom? And for how long? What mitigation is there?" Have your team prioritize and ask, "Which risk is most important today?" The priority and the impact of a risk today may not be the same tomorrow. A team needs to maintain an ever-evolving situational awareness.

In the Army we had a process of providing information in the form of the Commander's Critical Information Requirement to help guide subordinates in managing their response to risk. We used it as a framework to prioritize. It gave us an idea of high-risk elements—the things a subordinate should wake me up for in the middle of the night. It told us what we needed to be super-attentive to that might not seem like a big deal but which might really have an impact on a strategic level.

For example, if someone forgot to transfer vaccine from a cooler to the refrigerator and all the vaccines were no longer useable because they were not maintained at proper temperature, that was a critical incident because it could have an impact on soldiers who needed that vaccine.

One of the things we learned in 2020 was the central importance of leaders speaking in one voice through an authoritative spokesperson. In the military we have a public-affairs officer who is the spokesperson for the organization or a particular operation. With COVID, our government's designated authoritative source for public health is the Centers for Disease Control. But in 2020 there were competing voices and sources of information. As our understanding of the virus was evolving information and recommendations were changing. We had one source saying something works, another saying it did not work. When nonscientists suggested taking chloroquine tablets to prevent COVID people took them seriously. At least one person who took an inappropriate formulation of it died.

I was remembering that when George Floyd was killed in May. That was just really a tough time. I found myself thinking, What has happened to our country? It was a time of uncertainty, and people were looking for leadership. People were finally seeing the institutionalized injustices that go on, the things certain members of our society need to deal with every day.

In a way the COVID pandemic is like the pandemic of 1918. Back then people were just as confused as we are in 2020. There were instances of suppressing information about the seriousness of the pandemic. It was during World War I and the government did not want to worry people. This is nothing new. It is only new to us.

An important lesson is that things can be in total disarray but you get through it. We will get through this. We learn in the military that you keep going, you just keep marching. You don't surrender to the emotions of the moment.

If you saw the graduation ceremony at West Point in 2020 it was a thing to behold. The leadership brought the cadets back after they had been sent home in March during spring break. As they prepared for graduation the leadership kept them in cohorts of 200 and kept them in areas where they could be tested and quarantined if necessary. Before bringing them back to campus they called the cadets and said, "Give me your temperature reading," and the cadets did it. In the rest of the country, you could not even get people to wear masks consistently. They'd say, "I don't have to wear a mask. It's my right to not wear a mask."

In 2020 you were taking care of your neighbor by wearing a mask. It made me think about when my roommate's belt was twisted—about being responsible. It is not about you. It is about the greater good of others and our nation.

# Brilliance Is Only Half of It

## Henry Friedman, MD

*Dr. Henry S. Friedman is chief of the Division of Medical Neuro-Oncology in the Preston Robert Tisch Brain Tumor Center at Duke University. He is the James B. Powell Jr. professor of neuro-oncology as well as professor of pediatrics, associate professor of medicine, and assistant professor of pathology at the Duke School of Medicine.*

*Friedman is known for his work in the biology and therapy of adult and childhood central nervous system malignancies, including high-grade glioma, medulloblastoma and ependymoma. He played a pivotal role in the use of Avastin for malignant glioma and is a member of the team using an engineered polio virus to induce an immune attack on glioblastoma tumor cells.*

*Together with his colleague Dr. Allan Friedman—no relation—Henry Friedman founded the Collegiate Athlete Premedical Experience (CAPE). CAPE is a program designed to mentor Duke's female varsity athletes with an interest in pursuing careers in medicine.*

*From his position at one of America's leading teaching hospitals Friedman had a front-row perspective on the ways the crises of 2020 challenged the nation's health-care system. It was an extraordinary time when many of the ways Friedman's profession thought about leadership were revealed to be derived from organizational conventions that either no longer applied or had become dysfunctional.*

*The medical profession teems with brilliant scientific minds. But that is only half the challenge, Friedman argues, in building the prepared organization. The other half is finding the right talent to lead the battle against a health-care emergency such as a global pandemic.*

*In 2020 the American health-care system was trying to repair itself even as it coped with an unprecedented pandemic. The concatenation of what Friedman calls plagues that overwhelmed the system was something that should have been predicted. And it was. Good work had been done in making the system ready for the crisis. But that work was ultimately disregarded. For Friedman a lesson of that experience was that, in a crisis, execution is everything.*

*Uncertainty and complexity are hardly unfamiliar in the medical profession. Certainly that is true in a field like neuro-oncology. Medicine is a business that values protocols. Leading through uncertainty requires conscious attention to protocols in the areas of risk management, planning and attention to culture.*

*Friedman sees specific needs for rejuvenating leadership in health-care organization, including talent selection, culture building and training. Central to a doctor's training is assuming command in conditions of uncertainty. For Friedman, the heart of that training is keeping the mission of service at the center of decision making. That, he is convinced, is the path to seizing the transformational moment.*

There will always be things that come out of left field. But I do not think anyone is ever completely prepared for a moment like the one we experienced in 2020. I do not think you can train for it as a leadership challenge. But if you follow the basic principles by which you have led your professional life you can bring into play at least a framework for how to handle something new and totally unexpected.

You try to anticipate what might happen. If you want to talk COVID-19, for example, pandemics are something people have worried about for decades. Go back to the 1918 Spanish flu and even before that. Or go back to polio. Plans were set up to deal with all the eventualities, with what could go wrong. And then for a number of reasons in 2020 they all fell apart. Execution is everything.

In 2020 we found ourselves in a catastrophic event that we *knew* was coming. There was a playbook for this pandemic, and the NSA was in place to deal with the early warnings. The CDC was considered the best place in the world to handle this kind of thing. And at each and every level everything fell apart.

The 70-page playbook was thrown out, the NSA organization was downgraded, the CDC was allowed to age ungracefully. If that had not happened we might have had 10 percent of the mortality we saw and an economy that was not falling through the floor.

The problem with the CDC was not even that the playbook was thrown out. Having a playbook is only as good as the people you have for executing the playbook. The CDC was never modernized. They went with a leadership that only had half the necessary ingredients. Half of what you want is someone who is really smart, of course you do. But if you do not have the other half—the qualities of leadership—it does not make any difference how smart you are.

What is the leadership recommendation? My first prescription would be, first, get access to the selection of talent. That way you are not picking invisible men and invisible women, people who do not get it. Get people who are trying to make a difference.

Try and change the culture. You *install* a culture. I still see patients with the health-care providers in the clinic, for instance. Doctors are supposed to be serving the betterment of humanity. We are here to serve. For lots of reasons in medicine that culture has been lost. Too many medical centers are going to a philosophy of the bottom line and not necessarily the excellence of the institution.

It is happening in academic medicine around the country, and it has an effect on the quality of medical care. For one thing, we find ourselves now with a health-care system that is too easily overwhelmed. There is a steady eroding of support for community health, rural hospitals, mental health.

There are other things a leader could do in a moment like this that would change the dynamics. We are increasing the number of medical students every year, for example, without increasing the number of residencies, so we do not have enough places to train people. We need to make the financing of a medical education more equitable so that someone does not have to choose to go into a specialty because they are coming out of med school a quarter of a million dollars in debt. Instead of, say, going into primary care where we are desperately short of talent.

You need passionate, committed leadership. What you do not need are arrogance and negativity. I have seen bad leaders around the country who appear to be blind to the missions of medicine. And when you are dealing with people such as these you cannot use the normal rules of engagement. They do not apply.

I am a New York City kid. My career has suffered at times because I have a big mouth. Sometimes maybe I have been unnecessarily blunt and to the point. I am not perfect but I am an optimist. I have to be an optimist because of the patient population I take care of.

There is no question that in terms of what I do in my field I am a believer in the power of hope. You do not go into a sporting event or a firefight thinking you are going to lose. You are focused on a positive endpoint. When I have made mistakes—which I have—it is sometimes been because I hired people who were incredibly negative, just not positive people in any way, shape or form. And they were encouraged to leave.

I believe the canvass is blank until it has been painted on. People in the Preston Robert Tisch Brain Tumor Center live by that motto. It is about the mission. It is personal.

There are always risks, of course, and in medicine there are two kinds of risk. The first kind is personal risk, like the risk for someone working in an arena like a COVID ward or the OR where things can go bad really quickly. You have got a lot of hands in an open wound, you can get infections, you can get cut.

The second kind is the risk you manage in the population you are taking care of. You follow the premise of "Do no harm." In other words, whatever you are doing, do not hurt the patient. Do not give them stress needlessly, even at those times when you have to deliver bad news. At every level of the team—from the students to the nurse practitioners and the PAs, to fellows and attendings—you have got to look and make sure the people you are supervising are dealing with the issues at hand in the right way.

I delegate and I delegate. And I expect that people will do the right things at every level. But there are certain points where you need to know directly about your risk. An example would be a patient who is so unhappy that they are giving voice to the way they have been treated. I expect to be told about that so I can step in. I want to be involved in sorting it out.

For example, there are a lot of people who want to go on our polio study. It is doing amazing things with brain tumors and it will probably do some amazing things for some other cancers. But there are some people who are just not protocol eligible. There is a way to tell people when they are not protocol eligible. Just saying "We cannot help you" is not a message I want to deliver. The message I want delivered is that this particular therapy is not going to be beneficial for you. But do not ever say, "We cannot help you." Instead, we say, "Have your physician contact me. I will give you lifetime consultative care to help you." Having done that for over 40 years I have never had a patient walk away feeling they were treated shabbily at Duke.

My mother told me to treat everyone like you want to be treated or like you would want your family to be treated. If you do that you will never make a mistake. You might still make a bad choice but not in the way you behave. It is very straightforward.

I do not know if we are at a watershed moment now. There is such an enormous attachment to preservation of what we think is normal.

In 2020 I heard a sermon in which the rabbi drew a lesson from the Israelites who left Egypt. The older generation wanted to return even though there was nothing but horrors for them back there. So they had to wander through the desert for another 40 years before the new generation was ready to make changes.

My hope is that when we emerge from this desert—from these plagues—we will emerge ready to adopt a new normal. Because the old normal is not acceptable anymore.

# We Were Prepared to Solve Problems

## General David M. "Rod" Rodriguez (Retired)

*In October of 2014 Rod Rodriguez was asked to lead 4,000 U.S. troops in Operation United Assistance, the U.S. effort to stop the spread of the Ebola virus in Liberia and the whole of West Africa before it had time to spread around the world. Part of his initial mission was to support engineering efforts involved in building testing labs and treatment units. It was, as President Obama called it at the time, a "whole of government effort." Dr. Anthony S. Fauci, director of the National Institute of Allergy and Infectious Diseases at the National Institutes of Health then as he was in 2020, was a partner with Rodriguez when the world contended with a different virus.[11]*

*"Things were falling apart and I was given the order to go," Rodriguez says now. "I had no idea what Ebola was. When the Ebola outbreak happened our intelligence preparation of the battlefield wasn't much. Our Paragraph 3 was pretty blank. What we were prepared to do was solve problems."*

*Rodriguez had been preparing to solve problems for decades. Since graduating West Point in 1976 he had commanded at every level across the United States Army, including assignments as commanding gen-*

---

[11] "The U.S. Military's War on Ebola." Russell Berman. *The Atlantic*. October 7, 2014.

*eral of the United States Army Forces Command and the International Security Assistance Force in Afghanistan. As head of the International Joint Command he was credited with planning the US surge in 2001 that began to change the terms of the Afghan war by raising the professionalism of the Afghan National Army.*

*"He's patient and tolerant," the Afghan Chief of Army staff Gen. Shir Mohammad Karimi said of Rodriguez at the time. "But most important he listens to Afghan ideas, suggestions and recommendations."*[12]

*Rodriguez holds a Master of Arts in National Security and Strategic Studies from the United States Naval War College along with a Master of Military Art and Science from the United States Army Command and General Staff College. In 2011 he was given the Abraham Lincoln Award, first presented to Major General Ulysses S. Grant, which recognizes patriotism and service to the country.*

*Since leaving the Army in 2016 Rodriguez has headed the strategy-advisory firm DMR Consulting. In addition to work for Harvard, the University of Indiana, Rand Corporation and the African Center for Strategic Studies Rodriguez is also a senior fellow for the National Defense University. At the Army War College he teaches strategic leadership to classes of two- and three-star generals. He is a board member of Angel Wings for Veterans, Creative Associates International Global Advisory and The Leadworthy Foundation.*

*What these experiences taught, says Rodriguez, is that prepared leadership means being ready for challenges—often plural and at the same time—that one may never have faced in the past. The words adapt and adjust come up in his conversations a lot.*

*"You train for certainty and you educate for uncertainty," as Rodriguez puts it. "To be educated is to continue to develop and grow your capacity to handle anything. Because anything is what you're going to get."*

*Rodriguez learned to bring that philosophy of the expected surprise to his approach to planning. As he puts it, "You want to get close enough*

---

[12] "David Rodriguez: The general who planned the Afghan Surge." Rob Moreau. *Newsweek*. June 26, 2001.

*to right that great leaders can adjust quickly when things happen that they weren't anticipating."*

*In conversation about leadership Rodriguez returns again and again to the necessity of continuous training and education. One of the chief distinctions he notes between the military's approach to preparing leaders and the corporate world's is the lowered emphasis in the latter sphere on continuous education for senior leaders.*

*The population of potentially great leaders is larger than many assume, says Rodriguez—if they have the example of good teachers. He points, for example, to the multiple crises of 2020 as a teachable moment, an opportunity to draw lessons from a year when it seemed like nothing went as planned.*

*"Some leaders are great teachers in a crisis," Rodriguez remarks. "They take the time and sometimes unending patience to teach and talk about things they learned in the past but also about what they're learning as they go through the new experience. People remember those lessons for the rest of their lives."*

*Rodriguez likes to call leaders dealers in hope, people who can bring out resilience and perseverance in the teams they lead.*

*"Resilience has got to be a part of everybody's leadership capacity," he says. "You're going to have to figure out how to overcome failure and continue to look forward. The only reason to look backward is to figure out the lesson you need to learn from the experience. Everything else is moving forward."*

When somebody asks what a prepared leader is prepared *for* I'm not sure you'd get the same answer from everybody. From my point of view it's being ready for an array of challenges you may never have faced in the past.

In 2014, for example, there was the Ebola outbreak in Liberia. Things were falling apart and I was given the order to go down there. I had no idea what Ebola was.

In the military we always talked about intelligence preparation of the battlefield. When the Ebola outbreak happened our intelligence preparation of the battlefield wasn't much. Our Paragraph 3 was pretty blank. We had to learn quick and adapt to what we were learning. What we were prepared to do was solve problems. We were prepared to figure out what was going on and then make our plan and adjust as we went.

The first people who went to Liberia, besides leadership, were people from the intelligence community and people from logistics. It took a while to gain a situational understanding about what was going on. We were fortunate in having a big network of people who came to help us understand. What changed everything was the medical outreach and the communications to the trusted leaders of communities—religious leaders, tribal leaders, medical people. The communications piece was crucial to success.

After about nine or so months we were doing really well. But communicating the drop in transmissions when we went to the big meetings wasn't always easy. I had a young intel captain who created a hotspot map of all the changes in transmission. It was built on his experience making IED hotspot maps in Iraq. It showed we were in great shape—transmission rates were going down, hotspots were shrinking. Everyone got it. After that they could hear what the people from the CDC were saying.

In Liberia I listened a lot. I learned a lot. We continually adapted and tested. Some of the lessons of that experience would apply to the coronavirus but some are significantly different.

In any situation there's a group of things you know. There's another group of things you don't know but that you need to. That second group is bigger than it used to be. And then there's a third group of things you need to understand about the things you don't know.

In the coming decades we'll need better prepared leaders than the last generation. We're going to have to make decisions with imperfect knowledge or a lack of knowledge. We're not too good at predicting the future so we'll have to be adaptable and learn quickly.

Too much of the time we want to believe one situation is like another when it's not. Sometimes in managing risks there's a temptation to over-categorize things, to put things in boxes where they don't necessarily fit. Do that and you might miss a huge part of the differences between Ebola and COVID-19 and the responses you need for each. We want things to be simple when none of it is simple.

I don't think I've ever executed a plan that was executed exactly as we made it. You train your organization to execute in uncertain situations. You're getting it to think outside the so-called box. You want to get close enough to right that great leaders can adjust quickly when things happen that they weren't anticipating.

Wargaming or disaster gaming are a great help. They're a great training and education exercise. Red teaming—where you have someone whose job is to challenge your plan—is another helpful approach for the same reasons. And you can try to leverage the wisdom of crowds, as they say. From 30 different experiences you can see all the pieces of what the problem you have on your hands really looks like. In uncertain times the ability to bring those disparate perspectives together is a tremendous skill.

Anything is good that helps leaders prepare themselves for when things happen that are outside what most people were expecting. That is what's going to help them survive. If you haven't thought of those branches and sequels you should. The ability to adapt and change is the important thing.

You train for certainty and you educate for uncertainty. To be educated is to continue to develop and grow your capacity to handle anything. Because anything is what you're going to get. You're always going to be a little bit surprised. When you're a young leader the problems are more certain. That changes significantly as you go up. You've got to adjust your leadership and decision-making style to adapt.

From the start in the military we had continuous leadership training. At the Army War College, for example, I teach three-stars. Even if a subject is an ingrained part of your professional life you're still learning all the time.

What happens in the civilian world, in my experience, is that people who end up leading are the ones who do an incredible job of *self*-development. By that I mean experiential development but not too much institutional training. Certainly self-development becomes more important the more senior you get. But you also need the institutional training and education.

We all come to our jobs with a basic set of skills and knowledge and attributes. But we can all be trained and educated and grown into good leaders. How that happens is a combination of things. Setting an example is a big part of it.

Think about the experiences our nation was going through in 2020. These were what we used to call teachable moments, times when things don't go the way we want. In moments like that too many leaders just keep doing everything themselves. But some leaders are great teachers in a crisis. They take the time and sometimes unending patience to teach and talk about things they learned in the past *and* about what they're learning as they go through the new experience. People remember those lessons for the rest of their lives.

The military has institutionalized what it calls the after-action review. The idea is to describe what went wrong and what could have been done differently. You review what happened to figure out *why* it happened. The *why* gets you to the root of your challenge. There's an art to doing it so that you can bring information to the forefront.

In an after-action review seldom do you find out something was done out of stupidity. In the majority of cases you find out you had a communications problem. The decisionmaker made a choice based on limited information or sometimes bad information. Or there was a breakdown in the support that was supposed to be coming. It's never a simple answer. There are always a lot of moving parts. But you'll learn a tremendous amount. You can adjust.

In Afghanistan we had a bad situation I remember all too well. A young officer lost several people on an operation. I can still see that young man's face. A toxic leader would have said right away, "Fire that guy." I wanted to figure out what went on first. Later the commander wanted to talk to me. The young man was there as well. He said to me, "Sir, we haven't really trained and prepared to that level before we came to combat." Just the fact that he realized that they were not prepared was painful. And I told him I understood that. And that it made zero difference to me right then. We were not going to dwell on that. How were we going to learn from it? My team had to get where it needed to be as fast as it could. You go through that process to be better prepared in the future.

The more you observe people in tough situations the more you come to conclusions about who you can count on. There will be people everybody thinks are great until times get tough and they're challenged. Where there's uncertainty an ill-prepared leader is going to ask for more information and more time to decide. If you *don't* decide then that's your decision: to do nothing. And that's going to create more problems for you.

Resilience and perseverance have got to be a part of everybody's leadership capacity. You're going to have to figure out how to overcome failure and continue to look forward. The only reason to look backward is to figure out the lesson you need to learn from the experience. Everything else is moving forward.

All of us need to fight that reflex to worry about what's happening right now. A short-term vision just keeps jacking people around.

I do a lot of coaching and part of it is always about time management. I find so many people focused on what I call five-meter targets. They're in the present every day and don't give themselves the chance to separate and think long term. They're overscheduled doing a bunch of things that won't make any difference. They're never going to have time to *think*.

A leader is a dealer in hope. There are dark days and everyone needs to know that. But they need to be convinced that we're moving toward a brighter spot. I always smile when I hear someone called an inspiring leader. Because a leader had better be inspiring. But it can be lonely. There are just not a lot of people who are working on the same things you are.

Somewhere somebody is being faced with a situation that most would say is impossible, and they don't have many choices on how they're going to *make* it possible. When you're an old leader you'll want to be able to look back and say, "I got them prepared well enough. But they're not going to be perfect."

# You Learn to Read a Room Quickly

## Kenard "KG" Gibbs

*Throughout this book we have moderated a debate about whether the character traits evident in prepared leaders can be taught or whether they are acquired as a function of upbringing and experience. KG Gibbs is firmly in the latter camp.*

*Gibbs grew up on the South Side of Chicago, learning early to scope out his safest route between home and school. Later he attended Williams College and graduated with the intention of becoming a banker. But he soon left finance for the advertising world, joining Leo Burnett's Chicago office where he had accounts like Miller Beer, Marlboro and Sealey Posturepedic. While still with Leo Burnett Gibbs earned his MA from the Kellogg School.*

*Still barely 30 years old Gibbs was recruited to* Vibe, *at the time one of the hottest titles in the magazine business and the bible of hip-hop culture. From its beginnings* Vibe *was meant to be more than a magazine on paper.* Vibe *lived on multiple platforms including VIBE on Demand, branded CDs and DVDs, film and television.*

*The 1990s were the beginning of a crisis period for old media, and Gibbs' experience at* Vibe *would be preparation for his later transformation of established brands including* Jet, Ebony *and* Soul Train. *After the acquisition of* Soul Train *in 2008, for example, Gibbs revived the relevance of that classic American brand by developing content-distribution platforms like the Soul Train On Demand channel, SoulTrain.com, live events and international merchandising deals.*

*Experience has given us a fascination with character under pressure. As Gibbs puts it, "There are people who wither in the face of pressure and people who rise to it. Until you're in a hard situation you may not know who is who." The difference matters, he says, because "in a crisis you don't need to be the smartest person in the room. But you need to be surrounded by smart people."*

*For Gibbs, a prerequisite of prepared leadership—especially in advance of crisis—is an openness to diverse voices, whether at a board level or a senior-management level. Most people would nod in agreement with him. But Gibbs has stories to tell of leaders whose egos got in the way of hearing good advice.*

*Gibbs is quick to credit good advice when he's received it, specifically that of his mentor, Clarence Avante, a legend in the film and music business since the 1960s who overcame what in 2020 we called systemic racism: poor education, insufficient access to capital and the cold shoulder of mainstream media. And Avante succeeded anyway.*

*"No one likes crisis," says Gibbs. "But crises like the ones we had in 2020 can make people focus on issues. A crisis shows us where we have blind spots."*

There are lessons in leadership that are not necessarily learned from a textbook. You learn them because you've been in situations. You learn to read a room and read a situation quickly.

When I was about thirty years old I was recruited from the Leo Burnett advertising firm to join *Vibe*, the hip-hop magazine started by Quincy Jones. *Vibe* was about all the ways hip-hop was transforming culture in the 1990s. After several years I was asked by Quincy to come to New York to head up the magazine. I was charged with managing a group of about one hundred burgeoning journalists who were the voice of hip-hop culture. They were mostly kids. There were times when I felt like an RA in a college dorm.

I was charged with taking the magazine beyond print into television. We had a syndicated television show, and then we began producing award shows. In 2004 the *Vibe* Awards were in LA. We were in the Santa Monica Airport hangar taping the show with Quincy and any number of celebrities. Dr. Dre was receiving an award when his archrival, Shug Knight, paid someone in the audience to start a melee. Chairs were getting thrown and Snoop Dog and Quincy Jones were onstage. It was a situation none of us were prepared for.

We had security guards to make sure none of the talent had arms or whatever, but a stabbing occurred. People were trying to rush out and there was a bit of a stampede. SWAT teams were being called to the airport.

Now, I was an executive producer of the show. I took to the stage and for me it was an out-of-body experience. It felt like I was kind of looking down on this whole thing trying to figure out the most logical course of action for what was going on. Thoughts were going through my head about people's safety. And about how much money had been spent to produce this show. From a financial standpoint I was thinking we had no alternative but to get it shot. So let's be very methodical and get people calm, get them thinking someone is in control.

I got a live mike, and after I corralled some of the celebrity talent in the room to help me, we got everyone calmed down. We were able to complete the show even though all hell was breaking loose. We got it done.

Nothing prepares you for a situation where you think you have all things under control but then the unimaginable happens. But something compels you. Maybe that's prepared leadership.

By the summer of 2020 I was managing an office of probably twenty or thirty people. We decided in the spring that everyone would be working from home. It was kind of the same thing as the *Vibe* Awards. You are giving people the sense that you have their best interests at heart, number one. And you are leading by example. You're not necessarily letting on that you might be just as baffled as everyone else—not *pretending* you have all the answers but demonstrating empathy to people. You're projecting, hey, we'll make it through this.

Even as an entrepreneur and having raised money and put deals together with other folks there are a couple of things I've realized. One is that in a crisis you don't need to be the smartest person in the room. But you need to be surrounded by smart people.

A diverse group of voices, whether it is at a board level or a senior-management level, helps you arrive at better decisions. If you broaden the experience of the people helping you make decisions you get more well-rounded options to choose from.

At Leo Burnett I remember once going into a meeting on a female-hygiene brand. And it was all men in the room. I thought that was the craziest thing. Wouldn't it help to make a better decision if there was someone in the room who had actually *used* the product?

Even in bad situations you listen to smart people. Ultimately if the decision is yours you are the one who needs to make it. But you're going to make it with the input of other knowledgeable people.

Some leaders are more inclined to do that than others. The ones who have a big ego are the ones who fail. Everyone needs to know they are the big man in charge. Then there are people who are less concerned with who is in charge than with getting to the end result. Everyone already knows they are in charge. They don't have to tell everybody.

Chemistry is probably the most important predeterminant of whether something is going to be successful or not. It goes back to understanding the strengths and weaknesses of everybody on your team. I am not asking a guy who does not know finance to be my CFO. Everyone does what they're supposed to do. Collectively we'll form a high-functioning team.

Leadership needs to be innately human. In times of crisis you need that quality. If a leader has that quality they will rely on it naturally. It is who they are, it is how they operate. It's not happenstance or luck.

It's a funny thing about pressure in a crisis. There are people who wither in the face of pressure and some who rise to it. Until you are in a hard situation you may not know who is who.

I think it goes to not being stuck and only seeing something in one dimension. To not being afraid of being creative and maybe thinking in a different way. That is kind of the way I've approached my whole life. I am always thinking, maybe there is another way. Maybe I've got to go through a side door, maybe I've got to go through a back door. Or build a tunnel.

I've probably been wired like that all my life. I am a Chicago native, born and raised on the South Side. The area I lived in was very segregated, very polarized. I had to navigate my journey from school or be chased home. In high school I went through four or five different gang territories to get from my house to my high school. I always had to be nimble in terms of being aware situationally. It's how I've lived my life.

*Vibe*, for example, was owned by private equity along with Quincy and Time Inc. The private equity firm decided they wanted out. We—myself, the chairman and a few other people—went out and raised money and put a bid in. It wasn't accepted. It was one of those experiences where you work really, really hard, you give an arm, a leg and a lung. And you don't have success. So basically I was out of a job. Someone else ended up buying *Vibe*.

And that is when I decided to start my own production company.

When you look at stressful moments in your life some of them happen *to* you and some of them you choose. After *Vibe* I raised a first round of financing from a microcap hedge fund with my partners Peter Griffith and Anthony Maddox. Things were beginning to hum a bit. We had some deals lined up with Showtime and Lions Gate. So soon I am involved in a meeting with another private equity firm. We're in the Chrysler Building in New York. We lay out a presentation—a vision of what our company could do with added investment. We were not looking for a lot of money, actually. The private-equity firm told us they thought we were on to something. But the threshold at which they invested and what we were looking for were too far apart. They were looking to put millions to work.

They were leading us out the door. And all of a sudden I blurt out, "*Soul Train!*" My two partners look at me, like, What is this guy talking about? I said to the private-equity team, "One of our plans for the future is an acquisition"—because they had said to us if ever we were interested in doing an acquisition we should come back. When I mentioned *Soul Train* they get all excited and said, "We'd be interested. Do you have a way in on that?" And I was like, yeah.

I had been having some conversations with a trusted mentor of mine, a guy by the name of Clarence Avante. People call him the

Black Godfather. He is a music executive and a film producer, and he knows what he's talking about. I got him on the phone and told him about *Soul Train*. And nine months later we ended up doing a deal with Don Cornelius.

Prepared leadership is probably 90 percent character formation and 10 percent formal education. We have all met people in our lives with little formal education but because of their character they are able to do amazing things. That's Clarence Avante. He probably has no more than an eighth-grade education but he has ended up being one of the most influential dealmakers in the entertainment world.

African American businesspeople have always been entrepreneurs. They've managed to have their own businesses and operate in a certain way because they've always been faced with constraints on credit and capital to grow their businesses. Don Cornelius, for example, was a man who had a vision for *Soul Train* and he was unwavering in that vision. He was a former Marine and a former Chicago police officer. He commanded a lot of respect. He wanted to create a Black *American Bandstand*.

When he started in 1971 there was a lot of social unrest, similar to now. Basically what *Soul Train* did was allow high-school students to leave school and come to the studio where they could dance. It sounds simple and it was. But it gave Black youths a feeling they could show the world their creativity. It went national in 1971 with the backing of another African American businessman, George Johnson, who had a hair product he was trying to sell. He saw *Soul Train* as a great marketing tool. And it became a national institution.

Another class of African American professionals are in corporate America. Many of those people develop a different skill set in maneuvering up the corporate ladder and they hit a glass ceiling—punching through that glass ceiling in some cases but not in others. They become frustrated with the organizations they're part of. They feel the systemic racism that keeps them from progressing as their peers have progressed.

If you are in media your risks are definitely greater now. Even before COVID the publishing landscape had changed drastically. When we were all young there were three major networks on television. All your information, all your entertainment came through those three networks. Later came cable channels that appealed to every niche. Now you have got every Internet community you would care to be a part of.

Social media is probably far more influential now than any other media platform. It shapes perceptions. Knowing what is factual or truthful is harder than ever. In 2020 we were all talking about how social media was impacting our elections. That makes my job of communicating in a crisis harder. The way you think about your risks varies in the corporate world based on your core corporate culture.

Now I'm working with Viacom CBS in my role at BET, which bought *Soul Train* in 2016. It's a very tightly controlled kind of organization. I report to a president. Whether it's decisions regarding personnel, let's say, or money I want to spend I'm clear about my limitations. Certain things I need to kick to another level to get additional perspective. In other organizations you're given a P&L to manage and you own it. The results are yours. No one really questions your decision making unless you're not able to manage. You need to get comfortable with that.

No one likes crisis. But crises like the ones we had in 2020 can make people focus on issues. Without crisis people resort to their steady state. But a crisis shows us where we have blind spots. Before 2020 things may have been quiet for a little while. But to a certain segment of our society the crisis had never gone away.

When we look back at 2020 I hope we will say that was the year we started a real dialogue to address racial and other social issues.

I think 2020 will be remembered as the time when the country was willing to realize certain things. The biggest being that our country was founded on a premise of white superiority. It was founded on slavery and its inherent white supremacy. We are dealing with the effects of that. If we acknowledge that we can move forward.

Our country can do this. America is a great experiment. In the evolution of this experiment we are reaching another phase of it, and we are going to be tested. Our democratic capitalistic system is going to be tested. We can engage in constructive discussion and come up with solutions and be a better place. I'm encouraged.

# Figure It Out

## Colonel Kathleen Ford (Retired)

*In 2014 Kathleen Ford's daughter, Alaina, founded scDataCom, a security-integration company in Savannah. Soon after, she approached her mother with the idea of serving as a strategic advisor, drawing on Ford's 26 years of leadership experience acquired in the Army Nurse Corps. By 2020 Ford had assumed the role of CEO and scDataCom was serving customers in 15 states.*

*Then coronavirus happened.*

*Every young company is vulnerable to existential shocks. For scDataCom, the coronavirus shock meant rapid decisions about its business model—leasing security equipment it had previously sold, for example, and accepting subcontracting roles. It continued growing.*

*The central job of any entrepreneur, Ford argues, is reacting quickly to abrupt change—just as it had been in the Army Nurse Corps. For the Army she'd run hospitals and health-care facilities in the United States and overseas, delivering babies and treating wounded soldiers. When she left in 2011 she was Deputy Commander for Nursing, serving as a member of the Command Staff that set the organization's strategic priorities. It was during this period that she coauthored "Leader Development Transformation in the Army Nurse Corps," a guide to the cultivation of what the authors called full-spectrum leaders.[13]*

*"Leaders in a crisis," says Ford, "can't wait for all the facts to be in before deciding. Leaders have to ask themselves, when do I have enough*

---

[13] Leader development transformation in the Army Nurse Corps. Funari, Ford & Schoneboom. *U.S. Army Medical Department Journal.* 2011.

*reasonable facts to determine my course of action and take accountability for the consequences? It's basic risk management."*

*Ford compares the specific experience of COVID-19 to the attacks of 9/11 in the way it reached into every life in America. The dominant characteristic of both events was violent surprise. At such moments, she argues, "Formal training gives you some tools for leading in a crisis. But if I'm candid I have to say I am much more of the opinion that there are innate aspects of leadership"—aspects, she says, that can't be taught but are acquired through life experiences.*

*Ford points specifically to her experiences as a military officer. Veterans-turned-entrepreneurs, she's noticed, "have similar ways of thinking. For a lot of us the crisis of 2020 was much like any other crisis. You had to act quickly and read the situation and forge a way ahead."*

*A second similarity, Ford thinks, is the military's emphasis on earning the trust of subordinates before crises arrive.*

*During the pandemic, for example, scDataCom's employees were classified as essential workers. Customers needed them to show up. Ford was well aware, though, of how fearful her team was of bringing the virus home to their families.*

*"The communication style we used with our staff was crucial," she says. "It was essential that they trusted us to pull out the essential pieces of information from experts. In effect we were saying, 'Here's what we're asking of you. If you don't feel safe doing it here are your alternatives. We'll work with you.' And to a person they showed up every time to every job."*

When they run a mission, special forces asks individuals to take great personal risks. They're deciding yea or nay on a decision likely to cause loss of life. That's an extreme version of a risk-decision matrix.

In the corporate world you're not talking about life and death that way. But there are elements of it, especially when the problem at hand is a public-health crisis like the one we had in 2020.

The life and death of a person's livelihood is no joking matter. If someone like me can't keep their business afloat people don't have a job at a time where there may *be* no other jobs. That's hugely motivating for a leader to try and figure things out quickly.

Obviously 2020 was uniquely catastrophic. Most Americans were affected by the crisis. In the future we may see a lot of other crises not necessarily like it but similar in the sense of scope and novelty. How to manage the unexpected and come out as unscathed as possible is going to be something for leaders to study.

In a moment of crisis people can be so paralyzed by uncertainty that they don't do *anything*. You can't get stuck in analysis paralysis. In a crisis you don't have time. You'll get left behind.

Leaders in a crisis can't wait for all the facts to be in before deciding. Everything is a risk-management decision. Leaders have to ask themselves, when do I have enough reasonable facts to determine my course of action and take accountability for the consequences? It's basic risk management.

Risk management has been a piece of every decision I've ever made, in or out of the military. For a health-care facility, say, there are huge risk-management issues. Everything you do could potentially involve consequences. How do you prepare yourself for knock-on effects? You hope those will be minimal but you can never be 100 percent certain.

When I worked in health care, we loved disaster planning—mass casualties and all that kind of stuff. We spent a lot of time at it. But you will never anticipate every risk. You can't plan for every contingency. Amid ambiguity you have to *function*. You have to quickly and confidently identify gaps that may prove critical. And then you've got to decide.

The military taught me early on that you're never going to have everything fleshed out for you. Paragraph 3 is frequently developed on the fly. But you're smart enough to learn and figure it out and stay ahead of the competition.

That's kind of what the crises of 2020 required of businesses large and small.

For example, think about the whole work-from-home phenomenon. What might have happened over decades happened overnight in 2020. Did anyone imagine a time when work wasn't happening in office buildings but was getting pushed to the living room with kindergarteners, dogs and clients that you had to reach remotely because there was no opportunity to be in front of them? What's your sales strategy for *that?* The whole way we do business had to be completely reconsidered.

Will the *how* of leadership change to suit the color of the crisis? Sure, it always does. It builds on what we've learned. The way we work and the places where we work change. But the essence of good leadership won't ever change.

COVID resembled the impact of 9/11. After 9/11, every house in America felt the impact. COVID was the same. We had to adapt to an unforeseen crisis. We had to look in our toolkit and see what was in there that would help us navigate.

One thing I'll remember about 2020 is that I found strength in other veterans who had also become entrepreneurs. We have similar ways of thinking. For a lot of us the crisis of 2020 was much like any other crisis. You had to act quickly and read the situation and forge a way ahead.

We have impressed upon us in the military that at the end of the day our job is leadership. People who come out of that training are uniquely prepared to succeed in other arenas.

There is absolutely a different life experience being in the military that shapes what you think leadership is. It might be that the motivation behind leading is a little more pure in the military. What I mean is that there is not much incentive for personal gain, certainly not a huge monetary incentive. People don't necessarily earn more if they outperform others unless you consider future promotion. That's not a really big factor in performance. If you take away compensation as a motivator you get to the other things that motivate people to serve. You have a singular mission of service. *Servant leadership* is a term we used all the time.

In general, when it comes to character and leadership there are people who just *get* it. *Getting it* requires things you can't teach in a classroom.

Formal training gives you some tools for leading in a crisis. People can be taught doctrine, of course. But if I'm candid I have to say I am much more of the opinion that there are innate aspects of leadership. Compassion, for example, is an essential leadership quality that I don't think you can teach. It's something hardwired in people.

There are leadership skills that can be honed. But sensitivity, the ability to get into someone else's head and live their perspective? A lot of that can't be taught. It's acquired through life experiences.

In my military experience I was a nurse. Nursing is a service calling. In my business experience it's been the same. I have interactions every day with partners, other contractors, customers and a whole host of other people besides my employees. It seems it's easy to get a *Wow!* from people by delivering leadership that in the military I would consider ordinary.

As a leader you play the cards you're dealt. Military people are not all perfect performers. But the military has a strong emphasis on developing or realigning subordinates by either giving them more training or a different job where they can succeed. You're constantly assessing skills against a mission somewhere where those skills can be actualized.

In the civilian sector you're not compelled to do that. You can just move on and find somebody new to fill the space. Those with weaknesses can be discarded and exchanged for somebody new. There's not the need to invest heavily in the development of others.

In the military we worked on weaknesses to become strengths. When you bring that into your civilian business there's a whole mind shift among those being led once they realize they are valued enough that you are willing to close gaps when gaps are identified. Rather than just dismissing them, in other words, and letting them find their way elsewhere.

Sometimes that's detrimental to the business. You may hang on to people who are not a perfect fit just because you always have. But it's a sure way of developing trust. If you are willing to be honest with people and give them tools to improve they're going to be very sticky and loyal. They'll trust that your word is truth.

The COVID crisis was one of those times when trustworthy leadership paid dividends for us. If you'll remember, as we rolled through March there was nationwide panic. There was a lot of misinformation around. It was hard discerning fact from fiction and knowing what protective steps to take.

Our employees were classified as essential workers. Throughout the pandemic our trucks rolled. The plus of that was that our people had work. The downside was that they were fearful of bringing the virus home to their families.

The communication style we used with our staff was crucial. It was essential that they trusted us to pull out the essential pieces of information from experts, that the experts were leading us on the best course of action and informing our assessment of the threat. In effect we were saying, "Here's what we're asking of you. If you don't feel safe doing it here are your alternatives. We'll work with you." And to a person they showed up every time to every job. They put their lives in our hands as far as the protective measures we put in place.

We had already laid the framework for a trusting relationship. So when the crisis came our communication strategy worked.

In that crisis it helped that I had a health-care background. I felt confident that I was equipped to analyze and provide good guidance on the situation.

At other times in my life, and certainly in my career, I have experienced imposter syndrome. Every two or three years the military loves to give you completely new jobs. A whole new set of skills is required.

When I was a relatively young officer, for example, I was promoted to major and assigned a teaching position. The Army was asking me to teach things I wasn't good at, like diseases of the musculoskeletal system. I said, "I'm not an expert in that." The Army said, "Figure it out."

That experience served me well throughout my career. It taught me that part of leadership is being better prepared than your audience, whoever that may be. You overcome imposter syndrome by doing your homework. Knowledge is power. Information is confidence. That transforms you from feeling like an imposter to feeling genuine.

Today I'm running a security company. Initially I felt a little incompetent to do so. But the same technique I always used in the military—figure it out, go learn what you need to learn—served me well. I've gone and got my certifications in three states and feel well qualified now to do what I'm doing.

The military gave me a flexible mindset for conquering the unknown, doing jobs where it's maybe not clear what the requirements are. In the civilian sector people tend to be pigeonholed: "I do this thing, I have this skill, and I do it in this environment." That's not what an entrepreneur needs. It's much too narrow. As an entrepreneur you need to figure a lot of things out, and sometimes you've got to do it all of a sudden.

But be deferential to experts. That's going to improve your credibility. You don't need to be the final answer on everything. You need to understand the complexities and still maintain the leadership role. Be the smart liaison who is going to give your team the crib notes on the problem confronting them.

Perfect communication during COVID, for instance, would include a couple of links at the bottom of your emails saying, "Here's more from Dr. Fauci." Because you're not Dr. Fauci.

# The Job Is Supposed to Weigh on You

## DeMaurice "De" Smith

*ESPN once called DeMaurice "De" Smith's job the toughest in sports. Immediately after his election as executive director of the National Football League Players' Association in 2009, Smith began the negotiation of a new collective bargaining agreement between the NFL and its players. It was a historically contentious negotiation that ultimately provoked a 132-day lockout.*

*Smith and the NFLPA responded with a then-novel strategy of combining a legal attack on the league's lockout funds with a legislative agenda at both federal and local levels. The players pioneered the use of social media in winning fans to their side. Ultimately, they won a new agreement that included improved player safety, higher salaries (including a bigger slice of TV revenue), long-term health care, and better benefits for retired players. Most importantly, they successfully resisted the imposition of an 18-game season and a move by the NFL to eliminate pensions for NFL players.*

*Smith began his career as an assistant US attorney in the District of Columbia where he was primarily a violent-crimes prosecutor. He served as counsel to then deputy attorney general, Eric H. Holder Jr. He was later a partner in the law firms of Latham & Watkins LLP and Patton Boggs LLP, representing corporations, boards of directors and senior executives in civil and criminal matters.*

*In the winter of 2020 the NFLPA was voting on a new collective bargaining agreement when coronavirus took center stage in North*

*America. Even as the players were voting on their new deal Smith recognized that the impact of the virus on professional sports and American business was going to be immense. To Smith it presented a defining challenge for effective leadership by presenting perfect problems with imperfect solutions.*

*Against the desires of fans—and owners—eager for a return to normal, Smith and the NFLPA were convinced that conditions of uncertainty would persist not just for the 2020 football season but for an undetermined number of seasons to come. It was a fight against the urge to wishful thinking in the face of crisis.*

*As Smith puts it, "We had to bend our business to the virus instead of bending the virus to our business."*

*In tough circumstances the glamour of the top spot wears thin. The prepared leader accepts the weight that comes with the job. That includes the loneliness that comes with making hard choices.*

COVID-19 presented the most challenging leadership paradigm for anyone since World War II. Can you name another event that plunged everyone from CEOs to professional athletes, government leaders to small-business owners, into an existential conversation about their life and their future? COVID-19 put every leader in that situation instantaneously.

We represent all the NFL players as it relates to their wages and hours and working conditions. The relationship is codified by the collective bargaining agreement that the league and the players sign. In the spring of 2020 our union was voting on a new eleven-year agreement. The proposed agreement drastically improved salaries for most of our members and insulated pensions and benefits for generations of players. But it was an early deal and some members felt we should wait until the expiration of the current agreement to finalize negotiations.

We have 2,000 NFL players who are extremely young, full of testosterone and headstrong. We have superstars and journeymen, players who play a long time and some who have extremely short careers. The average career for our players is three and a half years. The injury rate is 100 percent. How do we protect them? I've got to figure out what a Tom Brady has in common with a backup long snapper and convince them of the reality of that. If I don't focus on the consensus piece there are more than enough things that will tear us apart.

An NFL coach is not thinking about an accountability structure for the best interest of his players over a long term. Coaches are hired and fired based on whether they win. Outside of winning a coach and a player don't always have aligned interests. That's neither bad nor good. It's just different. That is where the union needs to step in.

At exactly the time when our leadership team was discussing the merits of the proposal in Broward County in Florida the county declared a state of emergency for COVID-19. The basketball, hockey and baseball seasons were shut down. The NCAA's March Madness basketball tournament was canceled.

Before leaving Broward County I ordered John Barry's book on the 1918 pandemic, *The Great Influenza*,[14] which arrived at my house on the same day I returned from Florida. I finished it two days later on the same day our deal with the NFL was ratified by less than seventy votes. The book left me both terrified and inspired. It articulated so perfectly the state of our country at the time: slow decision-making, ignorance and rejection of scientific facts. But it also ended with hopeful lessons if we were ever again to face such a global threat. I highlighted all of them.

For example, both the Barry book and further readings on pandemics made it undeniable that COVID would not disappear. Developing a vaccine would mean several months of constant effort, if not years. The same history made it clear that quick, decisive action—masks and social distancing—could immediately slow the spread of the virus. Efforts to quickly identify who has the virus and quarantining them, along with isolating those who had been in contact with them, could capture and contain outbreaks. Leadership required blunt truths about what we did not know but also about what was within our power to change.

---

[14] *The Great Influenza: The Story of the Deadliest Pandemic in History*. John Barry. Viking Press. 2004.

In any organization the job of a senior leader is to provide vision and structure to a team. I quickly assembled a team of ethicists, epidemiologists, infectious-disease specialists and researchers to complement our internal team. We needed to answer two questions: Should we be playing football in a pandemic? If yes, how could we do it safely?

The *should* question was critical because football is not an essential business. I know many fans may disagree but it was completely unacceptable to engage in entertainment if it meant taking tests away from communities, taxing first responders or redirecting scarce medical resources.

Our COVID team was intimidating even to someone who has dealt with high-performing and demanding individuals. They told us the virus was novel, completely new and emerging. It would mutate and adapt itself to be more prevalent and deadlier. It was a perfect problem with only the hope of imperfect solutions.

At the conclusion of our first three-hour task force call I summed up my limited understanding of COVID-19 and football by saying that "if I have this right, the only place we could play football without contracting the virus is on an aircraft carrier or on the moon." No one laughed. There was no alternative universe where the NFL would not have a COVID-19 outbreak. It also turned out that I was even wrong about the aircraft carrier.

In every enterprise leaders deal with risk. As a homicide prosecutor and later as a trial lawyer I carried a confidence about my ability to win by convincing myself I had analyzed and planned for every risk. I handled cases for some of the largest corporations engaged in litigation involving billions of dollars. In almost every instance one critical question persisted: Had the corporation successfully engaged in risk management?

What most people don't see behind corporate operations is how successful companies transfer risks through insurance, offsets, contract language or other mitigation strategies. If they cannot do that there is almost no reason to engage in the business opportunity.

The hardest risk assessment was the core question: Was there a moral way to proceed with the season in a pandemic that did not place our members at unacceptably high risk?

The easiest risk-management challenge was reaching an agreement with the NFL to financially compensate members for the season at full salaries despite the looming drop in revenue. It required long-term financial projections in an uncertain market. We were able to manage that against a long-term collective bargaining agreement that provided labor peace.

For decades we had been through fights with the NFL over improved safety. Between 2009 and 2011 we drafted the first concussion protocols, hosted the first NFL audience for the researcher who discovered CTE (chronic traumatic encephalopathy),[15] insisted on baseline testing for our players, and endured shouting matches over changing NFL practices to decrease exposure to head trauma. When COVID hit we fought for the right testing, the right protocols and the modification of the season. We were under no illusions that simply because our experts counseled a particular course of action the NFL would adopt it.

I will always remember a call with our top players about the plan to play a complete season in a pandemic. Near the end of the call Tampa Bay Dolphins quarterback Tom Brady said, "It's the virus that's the enemy. We need to know how it attacks and protect ourselves the best we can while still knowing that many people will get it and we're not going to be perfect."

We had to think about what would happen when players and staff tested positive—how long they would be separated, when they would return and how we would protect the others. We also had to appreciate the likelihood that some might require hospitalization for COVID or other ailments. We engaged in an extensive analysis of whether we would lose too many players to justify the playing the

---

[15] Dr. Bennet Omalu. While working at the Allegheny County coroner's office in Pittsburgh Omalu, a forensic pathologist, conducted the autopsy of Steelers center Mike Webster. It led to identification of a new disease that he named chronic traumatic encephalopathy, known commonly as CTE.

season. Risk management began and ended with the humanity of the endeavor of football above anything else.

The success of NFL football is built on replicating methods of practice, precision, teamwork and sticking to tried-and-true models of performance. The downside is that change is something not always enthusiastically embraced. By admitting we wouldn't be perfect we were able to take the best tenets of preparation and apply them to something uncertain.

For a group of people whom fans may see as almost superhuman we negotiated opt-out salary structures and contract provisions for players who chose to not play. We made critical decisions early on to cancel the off-season program for most players and provided a structure for players who had salary implications for off-season workouts. We canceled the preseason games and restructured training camp. The goal was a complete season. Some preseason activities posed an unacceptable risk to that goal.

Knowing this would be a harder season mentally and emotionally on players, we pushed for them to have fewer hours on the field. We were managing and transferring risks by eliminating or modifying everything that posed an unnecessary challenge to the regular-season schedule.

In the end we reached agreements that engaged the virus with the goal of bending to it rather than trying hopelessly to bend it to football.

Study leaders through history and you see that no matter the quality of the team around them, tough decisions come down to one person at one critical moment. Lincoln faced a battle over whether our nation would survive as Americans turned on Americans. Before America's entry into World War II Churchill faced a Nazi onslaught that had more men and equipment than Great Britain could hope to produce. Getting comfortable with being alone in your decision making is something a lot of people don't get in their lives.

Early in my career I learned from the pressure and isolation of trying three to four shooting and murder cases per month and managing a caseload in the hundreds. I don't know many other things a person can do where you have so much hanging in the balance on your decisions. If I brought a case there was overwhelming evidence that the person sitting at the other table had killed someone or had done his or her best to take another person's life. It was important to make sure that person didn't have another opportunity to kill.

A trial lawyer wins or a trial lawyer loses. It came down to me. I made the decision about what witness to put on. I decided what questions to ask. I chose what to do during cross-examination. It surprised me how many prosecutors couldn't deal with that. They didn't like the engagement. They'd plead their case out. They couldn't live with being judged by a single event, win or lose.

A lot of people think they'd love to have my job. I get that all the time. The part of the job that's tough is after I get all the advice from everybody and then they all leave. It's usually on my drive home or the minute I lay my head on the pillow at night that I feel truly alone with a decision I've made or am about to make.

Becoming the kind of person who fits that role is a bit of temperament, a bit of training. You probably have to love the role in the first place. After that it becomes learned behavior. The loneliness of your position is something you either learn to embrace or you get out of the job. You have to deal with it or you can find yourself in a dark place.

It does weigh on you. It's *supposed* to weigh on you. If it's not weighing on you I have a hard time understanding how you're doing your job in the most thoughtful way.

There is isolation in leadership. But there is also mission. Ours is to represent our membership. There will be fights with ownership, and because of that there needs to be an understanding by our membership that we are all in this together.

My father was a Marine, and he taught me how to get through bruising fights by focusing on the mission and dealing with distractions without making excuses. My mother put herself through a segregated nursing school because she wanted a better life for her kids than the one she had as a child. Both of them exhibited class and a tremendous amount of resolve. Fights will happen, whether it's (NFL commissioner) Roger Goodell and me butting heads on health care or the anthem or player discipline. But there is no shying away from the fights.

# A Quality Beyond Resilience

## Sergeant Major Chris Donohoe (Ret.)

*Sergeant Major Chris Donohoe (Ret.) is a cofounder of EX-IQ in Raleigh, North Carolina. Started in 2018, EX-IQ employs artificial intelligence and machine learning to allow users to convert diverse kinds of content into interactive audio.*

*Prior to launching EX-IQ, Donohoe served 21 years in the U.S. Army, the last 17 with an elite special operations unit. That experience placed him in multiple senior leadership positions and gave him deep experience in the geopolitical challenges confronting the United States, especially in the Middle East and North Africa.*

*Donohoe has experience in counterterrorism operations, clandestine reconnaissance, organizational development, strategic planning, diplomacy and classified-data management. He holds a Master of Arts in Global Policy from Johns Hopkins University and a Bachelor of Arts in Political Science from the University of Northern Colorado. He is a winner of the Pat Tilman Scholarship and a recipient of the prestigious US Special Operations Command's Dick Meadows Award for Heroism, as well as the Silver Star for valor. He is a seven-time recipient of the Bronze Star, including two Bronze Stars for valor.*

*In his role as founder Donohoe's conception of prepared leadership—specifically in this age of uncertainty—is inevitably shaped by his military experiences. He is a reflexive contingency planner, for example, always on the alert for surprise. Even more central is his focus on people. It is a trait that comes up, for instance, in assessing the kind of talent suited to the uncertainties of a startup, with all its demands for regular reappraisals of operational premises.*

*Donohoe's experience has given him an appreciation of the intangibles that make a leader. Against conventional wisdom, Donohoe has come to believe that certain personality traits of great leaders appear to be inborn—good instincts, for example, or the personal charisma that moves people to do great things. Past some critical point, he thinks, those qualities cannot be taught.*

*Donohoe bucks conventional wisdom in other ways. He challenges, for example, the idea that collaborative leadership is the universal ideal of organizational cultures. Being an autocratic, hyperaggressive perfectionist, he jokes, is not always and everywhere toxic. Depending on context, it is a style that can be critical to mission success.*

*Make the mission your one obsession, your prime directive, as Donohoe puts it, and people will follow. But fail to put mission and people first, he says, and the organization will know immediately. Especially when times get rough.*

In 2017 I won the Pat Tilman scholarship and went to Johns Hopkins University. I was living in Fayetteville and commuting. Johns Hopkins has a foreign-policy school that is highly regarded globally. It was an executive program over 18 months, and I was commuting to DC every other week. It was pretty rigorous, and as I tell everybody, it took about three weeks for it to dawn on me that wife, kids, school and job left very little time to do homework.

I was on the road one day and I was about two weeks behind on my reading. One of the books I was assigned had an audio version. Cruising down the road I kept hearing nuggets of wisdom in that book that I could use for the paper I was writing. But by the time I got into DC five hours later those thoughts had come and gone. I found myself thinking, Why can't I take all my curriculum, convert it into audio, and interact with it as if I'm sitting at my desk? Highlighting, tagging, cutting and pasting, embedding comments and sharing? With millions of people commuting and on the go in our information economy to me this was an idea whose time had come.

I was introduced to an awesome technologist named Darren Ward, who came out of Microsoft to become my cofounder in 2018.

We created EX-IQ to take any text, any digital document or pod-cast, and convert it to interactive audio. In the 1.0 version we used machine learning to interpret things like headers and footers, strip them out of a document and then deliver the body of knowledge in that document. Now we're using AI to allow users to query, say, a hundred-page document for only pieces that are relevant to them. So a hundred-page document for the user is now a two- or three-page document of hyper-relevant content. It's pretty cool. We are creating a future that is inevitable.

A lot of us who spend twenty-something years in the military don't appreciate the mindset we come out with and how it helps in business. What the military gave me was a reflex for contingency planning. When it's life-and-death stuff and you haven't thought about something there are consequences.

A big part of my past was trying to anticipate the enemy's most likely course of action and their most deadly course of action. These days before critical meetings I run through that same mental exercise. I'll be on the phone sometimes and find myself thinking, Guys, how do you not see this as a potential outcome? We have to think about it, we have to plan about it.

The other thing that's useful to a startup is my experience lead-ing people in the military. When you have to lead people in circum-stances that are life and death you get a pretty pronounced sense of what makes humans tick and what they respond to. Startups don't have the biggest resources. You can't afford to go out and hire the biggest talent. So you'd better attract people with talent who want things other than monetary compensation.

When you're evaluating talent you see intangibles that give some people a real advantage. When I joined Delta Force, for instance, they kept saying our guys are intellectually curious. Intellectual curi-osity bakes in innovation and problem solving. When it shows up you're at an advantage.

There are certain qualities people can be taught but others, I think, are innate. Two people could have roughly the same set of experiences yet one of them makes ten times more out of what they live through. Could someone have manufactured Winston Churchill and his way with language? Could someone have manufactured Martin Luther King Jr.? No. And those people moved human beings. That's a big part of leadership.

There are times when you find that what you believed is no longer correct. That's when you have to challenge your premises. In the startup world that's the notion of a pivot. There are decisions you make even as a strong leader that, once you've made them, you can no longer influence. I think my previous experience gave me an appreciation for instinct as a factor of confidence in my own judgment.

There are mental models and frameworks for decision making that are helpful and effective. But above all else I think instinct is what I rely on. If you have an analytical mind and you've worked through the problem, if you've been thorough, you're left with your instinct. You learn to trust it.

I'm not convinced the world in the next five years is going to change as profoundly as some people think due to COVID. What will probably persist at some level is the remote distribution of the workforce. That's going to mean you'll need the skill to scale and inspire a distributed organization.

In the military I had the advantage of basically living with the people I was asked to lead. In the corporate world you can be very separate from the people you're trying to inspire. Either way you have to figure out how to inspire people so they bring their full talent to bear. Otherwise it lies dormant and people just go through the motions.

Full buy-in produces incredible results on the battlefield. Simply following orders far less so. Even in the military you might be surprised at how creative soldiers can be at slow-walking your intentions. If you've built a foundation, if over the course of a year or more people see you making decisions that have their best interests at heart, then when something pops up that they don't like they are much more willing to give you the benefit of the doubt. Because you've built up a track record. People trust you if you've done the right thing by them.

But people are smart. If they see there's something other than the obligations to the mission at work in your decisions then that's trouble.

I remember an experience in the Iraq war, for instance, during the mid-2000s. There was a lot of pressure coming from above at the time to have an impact beyond what we were already doing. One night the stars aligned to do that. I was in charge of the operation. When we got into the target area conditions tactically were less than optimal. The tactically sound decision—not going in—would have been the wrong thing to do for the health of the overall mission. We had to press on. It ended up working out. I had my team's trust.

If you're a startup you're vulnerable 365 days a year—ten times so when you're in a global pandemic. When the COVID crisis hit I was talking to one of our investors, the head of a multibillion-dollar real-estate company. He reminded me that in a crisis there are always opportunities. The economy was in freefall but I could tell he almost relished the challenge. It was a quality beyond resilience. It was what you might call being aggressively anti-fragile. He was determined that his organization was going to come out of this and probably better than before. He'd find a way to get it done. I've seen that leadership trait produce massive results in the military, and it did here as well.

In conditions of uncertainty the biggest thing for a leader is knowing what your "prime directive" is. In the military it's the mission and the team, the unit's integrity and its success. The military profession lends itself to these higher ideals. That's probably an advantage for creating a culture. At times in business ideals may get crowded out by the bottom line.

As a leader there are times when you have to decide on your own. There are other times when you have to have a conversation. In 2006, for example, I was serving a tour in Iraq. That was a moment when the prestige and the reputation of America was in many ways on trial. Like it or not, we'd engaged in a preemptive war that was not going well.

The crisis for me came when President Bush lost his majority in Congress. You had the leader of the US Senate saying the war was lost. There were indications that the fight in Iraq would be ended politically rather than on the ground. At that time the insurgency was adapting and we were unfolding new tactics that were not yet high payoff. But we had to get out there and continue, to keep the pressure on the insurgency. It was a contest of wills.

If there was a higher likelihood of someone getting hurt or killed than of mission success, and if it might all be for nothing, where did that leave me as a leader? It was a bit of the "last man to die in Vietnam" calculus. Political decisions were pulling me toward a lower level of aggressiveness to protect the guys. But at the same time, if we decided to dial back our aggressiveness there would be a steep price to pay in the streets for the Iraqi people because the killing would go on unchecked.

We got together as a team to talk about our obligations to the mission, to the unit, and in my mind, to the Iraqi people. It was clear that our prime directive was the broader mission. So we continued at a high level of aggressiveness.

If the team were opposed to what I felt we needed that would have been a leadership dilemma. But ultimately my decision would have remained the same. Part of the reason that didn't occur, I think, was that over the years we'd actively cultivated an aggressive mindset. From our core values I don't think we could have found a way to make another decision. But I found it important to air it out and let my people talk about it honestly. Having the discussion was its own good thing.

I've read a lot of management books. There are two I'd consider bookends for my collection. The first is Jim Collins' *Good to Great*. It's become a foundational text for EX-IQ. One of his big ideas is the "Level 5 leader" who has a balance of humility and will. Level 5 leaders are ambitious. But their ambition is first of all for the mission. They bind people to them by showing care and trust and building loyalty.

At the opposite end would be Ben Horowitz's book, *The Hard Thing About Hard Things.* He argues that there's no one best leadership style. There's a peacetime CEO and a wartime CEO. The peacetime CEO might use vulgar language but uses it purposefully. I know that sounds like bravado, something you might expect a military guy to espouse to further an image, but it's not that at all. I think Horowitz is 100 percent right. When the pressure is ratcheted up and decisions are basically existential for the company, the tolerance for debate is much reduced in the interest of time and forward movement.

It's good to be collaborative. But I don't fully buy into what some people call "toxic leadership." Being autocratic, aggressive, perfectionist; in certain quantities, yeah, those can be toxic. But business is a competition on a global scale. Look at Amazon, Microsoft, Apple, Tesla. If you read any history of Jeff Bezos, Bill Gates, Steve Jobs, Elon Musk, they sound a lot like what we'd call toxic leaders. But can you imagine the world without the companies they created? You could argue these are anomalies. Okay, but they are trillion-dollar anomalies. Leadership isn't an end unto itself. It's about output. That makes me think the conventional wisdom about what's toxic is incomplete.

The key distinction is whether those things are in the service of the company, of the mission. Someone like Steve Jobs, for instance, is clearly not a Level 5 guy. But he got people to follow him. He built one of the great companies in the world. The question is how he accomplished that. At some level I think leaders like Jobs are a two-sided coin. Their vision and drive are mesmerizing. But that comes with extreme impatience and unreasonable standards. There's collateral damage. But people are willing to tolerate a great deal to be part of something special.

# Hero Culture Doesn't Scale

## Neville Teagarden

*In addition to being a managing partner of AI Capital in Denver Neville Teagarden is cofounder and former COO of Lucid AI in Austin, a pioneer in cognitive intelligence. Prior to these ventures he held, among other senior jobs, CIO and CTO roles at Navigant and ProLogis over a 15-year executive career—a career that included responsibilities for technology venture transactions as well as M&A diligence and integration. It also included a term as director of technology architecture for Janus Capital Group, the giant mutual fund.*

*Teagarden earned his bachelor's degree in computer science at MIT, where he was also a researcher in the institute's AI laboratory. He acquired a practitioner's experience in developing enterprise systems across two generations of AI technology including analytics, semantics, robotics, machine learning and natural language.*

*Naturally, Teagarden is an optimist about the AI companies he invests in. The companies in his portfolio primarily develop enterprise software. During the coronavirus pandemic they were comparatively insulated from changes in business demand.*

*Teagarden was clear-eyed about the impact of the crisis on the world economy. But he also saw opportunity. Crisis, says Teagarden, is a revealing thing. And ugly crisis may be the most revealing thing of all.*

*The experience of 2020, for Teagarden, offered guidance in the prioritization of future investments. It is no surprise that health care and life sciences are high on his list. But so are companies that address global supply-chain disruption, additive manufacturing, streaming media and online retail.*

*"When you get a situation like 2020," Teagarden says, "that's pretty hard to prepare for. It helps if you've been through 9/11 and 2008. Those were major disruptions that created nonlinear change." They were good preparation, says Teagarden, for advising executive teams making decisions under uncertain conditions—which they are likely to be doing for at least another decade.*

*Teagarden is attuned to the character of the executive teams at the companies he invests in. The intriguing thing is that the kind of character required at different stages of a company's life cycle can change. The response to crisis can change too.*

*In its early days a startup may profit from the presence of a visionary who seems able to do everything. This creates what Teagarden calls a hero culture. The trap in hero culture is that it can be a threat to the mature growth of a business when processes have to be put in place that can threaten the hero's status. Adding to that particular challenge of growth, especially when the operating environment changes, is that the processes necessary to bring order in a mature company must not be so rigid that they fight the ability of the organization to respond intelligently.*

*"When a big crisis like COVID showed up," says Teagarden, "our portfolio companies pivoted to meet the change in the business environment. They did what we expected them to do."*

*No one can know the future. That does not mean organizations can't ready themselves for change—change on a massive scale, sometimes. If they don't, says Teagarden, they may find themselves surprised by a burning platform "fighting fires while trying to get things to change. That's a bad situation. It's why executives get fired."*

Crises are revealing things. They show you a lot about people.

There are the people who are reactionary, the same sort of people who sell their stocks on the way down and lose all the opportunity of a rebound. Because they panic. They want to act but they let their fear response take over.

Then there's someone like Carie, a woman I first worked with when I was CIO at Navigant. She came in a few months before 9/11 as a project manager in an application-development group. She had only some management background. When 9/11 happened we had to cut about 20 percent of the team within two weeks. I thought, "I'm going to use this moment to move this project manager in as a caretaker manager for an underperforming executive. We'll see how she does." There was something about Carie, leadership-wise. She was my biggest rock star in that whole situation. And then when I moved on to ProLogis I hired her to do something else when I heard she was available. She continued to more senior positions in her career. She emerged in a crisis and really stepped up.

When the pandemic hit we were fortunate with our portfolio companies. But there were some capital funds that made big bets in certain areas that weren't conditioned to an adverse event like the one we had in 2020. What they did was use the pandemic as a false excuse to reprice their portfolios.

You invest in a team as much as a product. The product will need to adapt to create a product/market fit. That's a big thing for us. When we're investing in companies we look at the executive team and assess its ability to pivot quickly. We like to see what's happened when things *haven't* gone well with the company before we invested, when it was in angel and seed rounds. How did it make decisions then? What did the team know when it made those decisions? And how did it execute afterward? Then we look at the results. That tells us whether the team is capable of changing.

When COVID showed up our portfolio companies pivoted. They increased revenue through the third quarter of 2020, month over month. We mitigated our situation enough such that, instead of losing a ton of money in the first quarter, our companies managed to pivot quickly and break even in the end. We're spending a lot of time with them talking about seizing the opportunity in the new environment.

They did what we expected them to do. Because they had shown that facility in the past. The kind of folks who can pivot recognize when change occurs in the environment. Sometimes that may require them to walk away from the lessons of their past experiences.

There are always minor crises going on. But a situation like 2020, that's pretty hard to prepare for. It helps if you've been through

9/11 and 2008. Those were major disruptions that created nonlinear change.

On 9/11, for instance, I was working in the travel industry. We were already under conditions of extreme high growth. We were not a typical *Fortune* 500 company. It was constant change and growth and stuff flying at you from left and right in those environments. So after 9/11 there were a huge number of unknowns. And we still had to make good decisions. As more information emerged we made more refined decisions or pivoted substantially. But we moved forward and adapted. We had to get comfortable with that.

Today, as an investor in companies, that experience helps me counsel leaders who have to make decisions under uncertain conditions. You expect people to uphold high standards. You have values you instill across the organization. When people walk in the door make sure to show that you care about those values.

A lot of people we interview for positions tend to self-select out. They'll be like, "Oh my God, I can't keep up with that." Others will say, "Wow, that sounds like a great thing" and start talking about how they've done it before. So interviews are about briefing them on what the environment is going to be like when they come to work.

It can come down to finding out who the perfectionists are. In a changeable environment perfectionists are not going to do well. To paraphrase General Patton, "A good decision made in time is worth far more than a perfect decision made late."

Before a crisis hits you've got to make sure a team is ready. If I were in private equity I'd be able to walk into a company and see if it had processes that enabled them to work across the corporation, if it were adaptable to its environment, if it could execute on change and scale up. When you're in venture capital, on the other hand, when you're at the early growth stage, that's probably the first time the company has had to start adopting processes.

At the angel and seed stage what you find oftentimes is a hero culture, where it's all about the individual skills of the leader. But hero culture doesn't scale. If something happens to the hero the whole thing fails.

Early-stage companies have a lot of generalists. Over time they tend to get good at one thing, but there are no backups for them. You start putting backups in place behind them once you've got enough scale. You manage risk that way.

As the organization grows heroes have to narrow their focus. Once you get to where you've got revenue, where you've got customers, that's when you start instituting process. The volume of work progresses to where there's a handoff. The handoff has to maintain controls so that that one person can't go rogue.

Your process has to be lightweight and adaptable. You don't need people who are going to put in hard-and-fast processes; there's that perfectionist gene again. It's not helping if you create policies that can't adapt to change. That's a big problem.

Even with the best processes you've often got behavior like passive aggression in the organization. It's like a sniper who hangs out in the tall grass, waiting. They choose a time to fire when it maximizes the damage. Or they just choose not to act, which is another form of passive aggression. It could be owed to ego and self-aggrandizement. Or it could be resistance to change. You need to weed those people out because they degrade the organization. Then the rest of the group can fall into cohesion again. Everybody has to be able to count on everybody else.

I probably don't explicitly talk risk management with people. I am more likely to talk about their authority to decide. You've got to be always asking yourself, What are the foreseeable risks? It's always about mitigation and contingency.

You don't know the future. But as you're approaching the place where things are going to start breaking you need to be anticipating. If you haven't prepped for change you're going to be standing on a burning platform fighting fires while simultaneously you're trying to get things to change. That's a bad situation. It's why executives get fired.

At whatever level, you're expecting people to think through their challenges and be ready to adapt. Then you can prepare at your own level.

An element I coach people on is about surprises and emergencies. If a surprise occurs usually it's a failure of risk management. You just didn't think about all the things that could happen. You didn't let me know the things you were worried about in advance so that I could respond. Your failure to plan shouldn't constitute an emergency to me.

Of course we do tabletop games, that sort of stuff. At Navigant, for example, when we moved servers from El Paso to Denver we played out all the decommissioning of the equipment in advance of making that move to figure out what could go wrong along the way. Another time we did a major cutover of a very large data-storage system. We did things like pulling the plug on it to make sure that our recovery scripts executed the way they needed to before we put data in the environment.

I can either surrender and say COVID is awful and the world is crumbling around me or I can be the inspirational leader who goes, "Well, wait a minute. This is how we're going to get into executing again and bring it all back to life."

# First Thing You Do for People Is Respect Them

## General Stanley McChrystal (Retired)

*Before his retirement in 2010 Stan McChrystal rose to the rank of four-star general during a thirty-four-year career in the United States Army. He served as commander to the Joint Special Operations Command— JSOC—in the mid-2000s. His leadership of JSOC is credited with the 2003 capture of Saddam Hussein and the 2006 location and killing of Abu Musab al-Zarqawi, the leader of al-Qaeda in Iraq. In June 2009, President Barak Obama and Jaap de Hoop Scheffer, the secretary general of NATO, appointed McChrystal commander of US Forces Afghanistan and NATO ISAF. His command included more than 150,000 troops from 45 allied countries. His last assignment was as commander of the International Security Assistance Force in Afghanistan.*

*When McChrystal Group was founded in January 2011 it was with the specific mission of working with clients to develop leadership solutions for organizations around the world, especially as they contended with volatile business environments. At its outset building stronger teams was the firm's central concern.*

*In addition to his role as founder of the McChrystal Group, McChrystal is an author of* Team of Teams: New Rules of Engagement for a Complex World, *which was a* New York Times *bestseller in 2015. McChrystal also coauthored* Leaders: Myth and Reality, *a* Wall Street Journal *bestseller based on Plutarch's* Parallel Lives.

*Since 2010 McChrystal has taught the popular leadership course at Yale University's Jackson Institute for Global Affairs. The study of lead-*

*ership has been a central part of McChrystal's life, binding together his service in the military and civilian worlds. Experience has persuaded McChrystal that the two spheres are different enough that the applicability of lessons from one to the other is not always exact. But in both spheres volatility creates complexity and ambiguity, especially as organizations scramble to adapt to the unknown as they did in 2020.*

*With that in mind, risk management has been a special concern for McChrystal in his evolving view of leadership in a volatile world. The pandemic of 2020, in his view, was a colossal failure of risk management.*

*In moments of crisis, McChrystal observes, bad risk managers punt. They pass responsibility to someone else, especially if that someone else is junior. They will say they need more information, even knowing that in moments of extreme uncertainty information may not be available— moments like those we faced every day in 2020. What bad risk managers are really trying to do, says McChrystal, is mitigate risk to zero, which he calls a Sisyphean task.*

*Even before the arrival of COVID-19 American society struggled with the absence of trust pervading social, economic and political relationships. When the pandemic erupted in March of 2020 the necessary trust to deal with hard problems wasn't there—a costly cultural deficit because, as McChrystal puts it, "in any exchange between people trust lowers transaction costs."*

*Especially in moments of crisis, McChrystal points out, trust is earned by owning mistakes, listening to our organization and managing our emotions. In a crisis trust can be squandered, particularly if leaders choose to ignore big problems and busy themselves with near-term issues that they persuade themselves are urgent.*

Leadership is already challenging but crisis makes it more so. In a crisis there are lots of temptations for leaders to delay decisions. They will say they need more information. That's not possible in moments of extreme uncertainty, like the moment we live in now. What they're really trying to do is mitigate risk to zero. That can't be done, not in a crisis and not ever.

When everything is going to hell the first thing to do is figure out if you've really got a crisis on your hands. There are moments that feel like crises that are not, so there is no point in panicking. There are other moments that may not seem serious but are. There is no denying it—to yourself or others.

Worst of all, sometimes you are the cause of a crisis and your fingerprints are all over it. There is a temptation to deny that fact, to maybe not tell the whole truth. Maybe you convince yourself you don't want to scare your team. But be honest: tell the people around you there's a problem. If you are responsible and you are in charge, you're going to hate the tension between those two things, especially if you are in denial.

Regardless of the cause of a crisis your job as a leader is to manage yourself. There is no room for panic, there is no room for losing your temper. Once or twice getting angry can feel good. But each time you rely on anger it will have diminishing marginal returns. From the outside you will come across as too emotional.

A lot of the time the challenge is separating the urgent from the merely important. A good example would be education in America. That is a real crisis. We can't fix education in America in less than a generation. But we've still got to start the work right away. There will be temptation to look at the near-term things coming at us rather than the bigger problem we've got to take on. Good leaders resist that temptation. I can't emphasize that enough.

No one at my firm would claim we foresaw the crisis of COVID-19. We certainly *did* foresee long-term consequences to the operating environment in the event of a pandemic. We extrapolated from what we had experienced in Iraq when deep uncertainty made tasks more complex and fundamentally harder to deal with—in some cases *impossible* to deal with as long as we relied on traditional solutions to new kinds of problems.

We formed McChrystal Group on the hypothesis that the experiences I had at, say, the Joint Special Operations Command, were not unique to the military or to counterterrorism. The civilian world turns out to be a broader environment. It caused me to evolve my thinking about what makes an organization work and what makes an organization fail. In doing that I looked back on my own long training as a leader, in the military and beyond. Every day there are things I wish I had known. And I mean every day.

I like the phrase "prepared leadership." The military does a number of things well to prepare its leaders. It teaches basic processes and procedures that can be applied under different names in other organizations, like restructuring and changes of command. Throughout your career those basics are reinforced. But they are maybe 40 or 50 percent of what you need to even scratch the surface of being prepared to face a challenge.

When you are a young soldier, for example, you might need a certain number of troops for a defined task. That's not wrong but it will be too narrow for what is required as you get broader experiences. When you get more senior in your career you deal with different parts of the government. Suddenly, you realize you're dealing with all these different cultures, different incentives, different backgrounds. It can be overwhelming.

In the military the culture of leadership, the culture of responsibility, the culture of dedication to a larger mission is powerful. The energy and the commitment these create let the military get away with a lot of other mistakes. That being said, the military is remarkably risk averse. You might say, wait a minute, how can asking people to do life-and-death jobs be risk averse? But from the beginning of our careers we learn you cannot fail the mission. Everything is belt-and-suspenders.

As military leaders, we are certainly risk averse to losing our people. Sometimes nationally we get so risk averse that we will not take the necessary risks to get the mission done. In Bosnia in the mid-1990s, for instance, the mission was not to lose anybody. With that central goal it honestly would have been easier for troops to just stay in the United States.

The military can get itself wrapped around the axle on risk aversion. You might think that once you go into combat the shackles are thrown off and people are fast-moving. But if you shape the culture of an organization to be risk averse and conservative it will reveal itself in those moments of fast movement. A good percentage of our senior leaders sometimes can't get off the *x* because they are so embedded in that culture.

Now it's not easy to compare that attitude to the civilian world where it is harder to convince the workforce that what they're doing is for the greater good of mankind. The metric is, historically, to make money. When you get into the corporate space you deal with boards of directors, you deal with incentives, you deal with bonuses and all the other dynamics affecting how people act.

But the civilian world is also decisive, much more willing to take a ninety-degree turn and go in a new direction at a given moment. You will get CEOs who'll walk in on a Monday morning and change their approach or perspective. A military leader would wring their hands for months.

If you could wrap the two cultures together you would have something pretty powerful. What is common to both cultures is the essential value of mutual trust.

In any exchange between people trust lowers transaction costs. If you trust somebody then you don't have to check what they say. You don't feel the need to guard or protect yourself.

You want to build trust? The first thing you do for people is respect them. You are only going to get followership if you build people's desires to follow you. If not, they won't do more than the bare minimum. Even in the military ordering people to do things only works to a point.

It's a funny thing about soldiers. If you listen to them and then decide something completely different, they don't really resent it too much. But if you *don't* listen to them and even if what you decide to do agrees with their own ideas, there will be a level of resentment. It is no different in a company.

You can't always explain everything to everybody. In a crisis you are forced to operate on muscle memory, on the legitimacy you built before the crisis hit. If you're pretty smart, have the right instincts and the right values, people will trust you. When it's time to do things that are really hard you will have earned the ability to say, "Okay, I want everybody to try this new idea" even though it may seem preposterous in the moment. If the level of trust in you is high you will get a lot more support than you might have expected.

Every organization I've ever been with views empowering its people as a problem to work on. They struggle to get people to make decisions, to take risks, to take initiative. Step one is that people should not fear getting hammered if they try things and make a mistake. There should always be a commonsense test that is legitimate for these new efforts. But that same test should not be a cop-out leveraged by senior leaders who have failed to give a more junior person the right kind of guidance.

I've found the civilian world is much quicker to fire people than the military. In the military there is just so much baggage associated with firing that it is something they almost never do. Some people should get fired, the same way you would pull a pitcher out of a baseball game. But civilians are too quick on the trigger sometimes. They think if it's cloudy today we'll fire people and that will make it sunny tomorrow. There's often much less effort to correct a problem than there is to *replace* a problem. In moments of crisis you need to focus on correcting the issue at hand.

That is what it was like trying to lead through COVID-19, I think.

Something you will notice that is characteristic of navigating crises is that there tends to be an abrupt formation of ad hoc organizations. You saw that in the US government for the COVID-19 crisis. People may know each other but don't deal on a normal basis because they don't have to. Suddenly they are working in this diverse organization. How quickly can they build up a level of trust and can get stuff done?

That is where many folks found themselves in 2020. There was so little trust in much of the governance of the United States, so little trust in institutions, so little trust even in science. That added friction to the process of solving our problem. People would make a decision and other people would second-guess it right away. As a result a lot of people were scared to make decisions.

We've all worked with people who create an atmosphere of mistrust. We've been in situations where someone is abusive. We've been in other situations where someone just is not realistic. You might get an entire organization speaking happy talk to each other while things are going to hell. That is dangerous because it prevents reality from being recognized.

Toxic leadership does not need to be yelling and screaming. It can be anything that prevents an organization from doing what it should do. If you are not candid with yourself and your team that is toxic, plain and simple.

Adopting this kind of operating outlook requires senior leadership buy-in. To be clear, they will struggle with it. We have a couple of cases where we were hired by big companies. The senior leaders were paying us a lot of money but the reality was that they were not engaged. Consequently, everybody in the organization kind of said, "Well, this isn't serious. This is just someone's pet project." There have been cases where we've had pretty active opposition inside the organization. Sometimes people felt that they were losing their power base.

You can overcome that if you get a critical mass of people involved. Without that, people just aren't willing to make substantive change. Nobody wants to be the person who burns a lot of calories on change and then finds out it wasn't necessary. That can leave an organization just sort of dog-paddling in circles.

The hardest times for leaders are when an issue comes up and their gut says they have got to go a certain way even though there is a significant amount of risk or a significant amount of opposition. In those times, leaders need to be able to say, "I've looked at all the data, I've consulted with the right people, and this is what I've decided." But you can't go to that well too often. It's a big ask.

There are times when you're uncertain and you have just got to act a part. That can be a first step in getting off the $x$, in overcoming inertia and moving out of your comfort zone. I'm not saying it's easy. But you can't let yourself or your organization be paralyzed by crisis, by uncertainty. You have got to get moving.

# It Gets More Bearable As We Go Through It

## Stephen W. Beard

*In 2018, the year Steve Beard joined Adtalem Global Education as general counsel, he brought with him a rich collection of experiences from senior legal roles. He had held the general-counsel job at the giant search firm Heidrick & Struggles, where he was a seven-year veteran. Before that he practiced law at Schiff Hardin LLP, specializing in M&A work. In 2019, when he took on the COO role at Adtalem, Beard could not have imagined how different his experience was about to be from what he knew before.*

*Twenty-twenty was the year Beard was recognized by* Savoy Magazine *on its annual list of Most Influential Black Executives in Corporate America. And it was the year Adtalem would find itself abruptly confronting a pandemic in multiple countries with the lives of employees and students at risk.*

*Being a comparatively new guy at Adtalem, Beard was glad for the support of the organization's existing crisis management capabilities. Operating in the Caribbean, the company had a well-developed reflex for responding to natural disasters—hurricanes specifically. But a pandemic was something new and dangerously different. It was much slower rolling than a hurricane and exponentially more threatening.*

*"As someone who'd only been with the company two and a half years," Beard says now, "it was interesting watching the team attempt to apply the framework to a totally different set of facts. It was a lesson in*

*being critical about what's applicable from prior experience and what's not."*

*A crucial test of prepared leadership is knowing when lessons learned in the course of a career have value and when they create a trap of misidentifying the novel nature of a crisis. Precisely because we worked hard to master lessons that served us well in the past we reach for them instinctively in crisis. Slowing that reflex is a test of self-awareness.*

*"We needed a totally different viewpoint," Beard recalls, "because we were going to be at this not for two weeks but for the rest of the year."*

*The value of the Adtalem's veterans was not discounted; on the contrary, they had developed best practice in internal communications, stakeholder relations and logistics that was enormously valuable. Beard and the other relative newcomers were able to serve as a kind of red team, challenging accustomed strategies—legacy thinking, in Beard's phrase—to make them better.*

*"In any setting," says Beard, "the idea of the omniscient leader who knows best is a problem. Leadership with humility unlocks the contributions of everyone. It opens a world of possibilities."*

*That was never truer than amid the volatility and uncertainty of 2020.*

*For Beard, who was named Adtalem's CEO in 2021, decision making during the pandemic and its accompanying social crises will be whether they served not just to navigate the moment but to position the company to be stronger than it was before.*

Adtalem, broadly speaking, is an education business. We operate in two industry-focused verticals: financial services and health care. We own the country's largest nursing school. One out of every 30 nurses in the United States holds a credential from Chamberlain University. We own two of the largest international medical schools and one of the largest veterinary schools, all three of which we operate in the Caribbean. We own financial-services businesses that train and certify finance professionals.

The pandemic created a lot of logistical challenges. It seemed as if, overnight, the pandemic disrupted our ability to bring people together for in-person instruction and events. It required us to migrate large portions of our businesses to virtual settings. That's not as simple as just putting people in front of a camera. It presented a lot of risks that required us to think with foresight.

We were fortunate because we had a crisis-management infrastructure already in place that predated my arrival at Adtalem. Operating academic institutions in the Caribbean we'd dealt with natural disasters before. We'd dealt with hurricanes and evacuating students and faculty. The organization had an infrastructure for thinking about stakeholder engagement in a crisis.

Those of us who were new had the benefit of what the veterans knew. We newer people were able to be the critical red team of the legacy thinking.

As someone who had only been with the company two and a half years it was interesting watching the team apply the framework to a totally different set of facts. Folks immediately, and naturally, fell back on their hurricane experience. That was the battle they lived through before. The pandemic was an entirely different type of circumstance for us.

Hurricanes are a fast-moving crisis with a well-defined set of potential consequences. The pandemic unfolded much more slowly. The consequences were not well understood because the *pandemic* was not well understood. It was going to be a moving target over months, not days. We had to take our experience with tropical storms and morph that to deal with the very different characteristics and variables of COVID.

Our crisis-management framework was a great tool. We knew best practice. We engaged our board of directors in thinking about public relations, for example, what we said and what we didn't say. We delegated tasks across the organization. We knew how to share information. We knew how to facilitate decision-making. But we needed a totally different viewpoint. Because we were going to be at this not for two weeks but for the rest of the year.

In our crisis playbook there is a directive about overcommunicating. We continually repeat the critical messages we want people to take away. We do it through multiple modalities. Most importantly we do it with empathy for the audience.

In a crisis situation the world speeds up. There's a temptation to speed up with it. You may need to resist the temptation to do something immediately—particularly when you're dealing with the fast-moving environment and limited information that a crisis brings. We did a great job taking a step back to think about the human challenge for each of the constituencies behind the logistics and focus on that from the perspective of reputational risk. From there we were able to address the most critical elements.

As a leader it was important to get people comfortable with a new kind of ambiguity. It was a lesson in being critical about what's applicable from prior experience and what's not. The leadership challenge was to ensure that the team wasn't so attached to process that it was not able to adapt to the crisis of the moment, which in most cases is going to be very different from the crisis of the past.

For example, there was the question of airlifting people out of the Caribbean. Their families were certainly going to be focused on that. We didn't want to bring 200 infected, or potentially infected, people from Barbados to Florida.

If we moved to online instruction, what was the implication for the perception of value our students were getting for the same tuition dollar? If we were no longer delivering instruction in person should we change the price of our offerings? What message would that send to the market? Should we provide financial support to students who were dealing with dislocations as a result of the pandemic?

When people look back on the choices we made in 2020 we wanted to be sure we focused on the right things.

Leaders are burdened by thinking ahead several moves. How does what we do now impact what we need to do in the future? How do I ensure that I'm focusing the team on things that meet immediate needs *and* incorporate what the future outcome needs to be? Managing risk necessarily requires you to look into the future. That's what we did.

During times of crisis the leader needs to set an example. It should be deliberate and conscious. If you're doing nothing you're still setting an example—a really bad one.

Where organizations and leaders go wrong is when they make sweeping long-term decisions on the basis of relatively small data sets. Have the patience in your own thought processes. Allow yourself the space to be deliberate in how you direct the team. Not only because it is likely to yield a better response but because it gives people confidence that in the heat of the moment the leader is not losing their head.

A big part of a COO's job is the integrator role. I spend a fair amount of my time identifying people to bring to bear on a given issue, ensuring they're adequately resourced and informed, facilitating their work in a way that serves up the best options for the organization. Once I've done those things my job is attention to the issues.

I think about making informed decisions sequentially: there is a place for collaboration, for integrating perspectives, for resourcing teams. But once collaboration is over you decide. You give folks reason to believe in your decision so they will go after it with the commitment.

My father used to tell me that every great leader lives a life of quiet desperation because there are a lot of people counting on them. It's a privilege to have people counting on you. There's a humility required to demonstrate the extent to which you personally are grappling with the challenges of the moment, that we're in this together. When people know you have *their* back they are inclined to have *your* back. They'll commit to the fight. That kind of trust you earn over time.

Little of what I'm describing comes from formal training, academic or professional. But I'm not someone who believes leaders are born. I think they are made in the crucible of experience and from the will to make the most of that experience. A lot of the way I think comes from opportunities I've been given by leaders who were willing to make a bet on me. They allowed me to develop an appreciation for leadership attributes that lend themselves to high performance in challenging environments, like the pandemic.

I'm managing teams outside the domain I trained in as a lawyer. When I became a general counsel I thought of myself as a better lawyer than most of the lawyers who worked for me. Then I moved into other areas like corporate strategy, corporate development and com-munications. I was managing people who'd forgotten more about those domains than I'll ever know. What makes me good in that context is a willingness to be the inspiration, not the perspiration.

I've also become comfortable learning from other people and taking pleasure in being curious. I may apply my judgment but I let other people be the expert. It's a sign of confidence and trust. Leadership with humility unlocks the contributions of everyone. Learning this opened a world of possibilities for me. During times of crises it is especially valuable.

Traveling the arc from expert to manager to leader requires you to drop the things you mastered and open yourself to mastering something different. That takes professional courage. As I continue to build a team I'm looking for folks who evidence a willingness to take risks by embedding themselves in a different context. When I am looking at people, thinking about their development, I'm inter-ested in people willing to bet on themselves.

Betting on yourself is a willingness to acknowledge that what got you to where you are is not going to take you to where you want to go. You need to take the risk of retooling, to be willing to be bad at something in order to become good at it. A lot of folks get to a place of mastery and become so enamored of what they've mastered that they just hold on to it.

In any setting the idea of the omniscient, charismatic leader who knows best is a problem. Those are not leaders focused on bring-ing people together in productive ways. They're focused on leverag-ing people for their particular agenda. For a time you can get away with that. But eventually organizations suffer.

Intelligent risk taking is how you create value. That's what a business is. Even in the context of crisis you're innovating to manage a particular risk. Your innovation may have applications to the way you run a better business on a go-forward basis.

Sometimes, when you get to the leader-versus-manager discus-sion, it feels disparaging of managers, which it shouldn't. Great man-agers are crucial for success. Managers should be objective-focused. If we're thinking about communicating, for example, good managers execute with the goal of overcommunicating. At Adtalem we communicate now at a pace far beyond what we were doing pre-pandemic. People need to understand what's going on so that they feel like part of the process.

Leaders are, by definition, people focused. In the current environment being a leader brings with it a tremendous weight of responsibility.

The human condition was under so much assault in 2020. You had the pandemic with all its public-health implications and death on a massive scale even in a relatively wealthy country like the United States. You had the attendant economic crisis that came from that. You had the reckoning with racial justice that arises every time we grapple with other crises. In their own way your people are grappling with those crises. Your ability to engage with them bears on your success in delivering for the customer.

For instance, for employees with families this is an incredibly stressful time. Think about remote learning for their kids—how can we be more helpful? How do we ensure that working in a home office is as comfortable as we can make it? How people feel is going to impact how they perform. We avoid long stretches where we haven't said anything about what we are thinking about the current environment or without a pulse survey to see how folks are doing.

What interested me about the pandemic was that its impact was exponential. What will be durable in that experience is that the pace of change—in normal times and in crisis—is accelerating.

The military often uses the term VUCA—volatility, uncertainty complexity and ambiguity. In the future VUCA will only become *more* VUCA. The nature of the challenges may differ. But the pace at which they unfold, the need to respond at that pace and the multiplicity of stakeholders who need to be addressed will only grow. There's your new normal.

The term *prepared leadership* will mean being ready to feel uncomfortable. We will have to lead with limited information and still be deliberate in a way that creates conditions for sound decision-making—even as the world speeds up. That is an individual competency. I suspect it's something that can be extended to organizations as well.

Organizations can be crisis ready. They can be prepared to be dynamic and to create conditions that result in wise decision-making. We were fortunate to have a crisis playbook we could fall back on. But what made us successful was a team dynamic of trust, humility, intelligent risk-taking, transparency and empathy. That got us where we needed to go.

I feel privileged to be in a position to pull some of the levers in a way that eases the crisis. It gets more bearable as we go through it. We learn. We will emerge a better, more competitive organization and, by extension, maybe a better society.

# What Raises You Up as a Leader

## June Ellen Ryan, Rear Admiral, US Coast Guard (Retired)

*June Ryan practices what she calls meta-leadership. It is an idea first developed in 2006 by Leonard J. Marcus and Barry C. Dorn of the National Preparedness Leadership Initiative in collaboration with Joseph M. Henderson at the Centers for Disease Control and Prevention.*[16] *What differentiates meta-leaders, Ryan thinks, is their behavior in a crisis.*

*Meta-leaders take a holistic view of any situation. In an emergency they transcend organizational lines in pursuit of a common purpose: beat the crisis.*

*Leaders, says Ryan, are shaped by crisis. Early in her career Ryan served aboard three Coast Guard cutters, two as commanding officer. She subsequently served as the military aide to the President, only the third woman in US history to serve in that job. In 2010 Ryan served as the Coast Guard's acting assistant commandant for response policy during the Deepwater Horizon oil spill.*

*Ryan's first assignment as a flag officer was as military advisor to the secretary of Homeland Security, the first woman to hold that position. She served during an unprecedented period in US history, developing*

---

[16] "Meta-Leadership and National Emergency Preparedness: A Model to Build Government Connectivity." Marcus, Doran, and Henderson. *Biosecurity and Bioterrorism: Biodefense Strategy, Practice, and Science.* June 2006.

*national policies and operational protocols between DHS departments across the US and foreign governments. During her time at DHS Ryan worked on several national crises including the US response to the Ebola outbreak and to the immigration crisis at the southwest border of the United States.*

*Ryan's final post was as the Ninth Coast Guard District commander in the Great Lakes and Saint Lawrence Seaway region of the United States. Her command included eight states, a 1,500-mile international border and a workforce of 6,000 active duty, reserve, civilian and auxiliary men and women. In a role like that being* meta *was a job requirement.*

*For Ryan, the defining trait of a prepared leader is not flexibility but what she terms* pliability. *Pliability, as she defines it, is a capacity to use the same raw materials that brought success in the past but applying them in wholly new ways to the crisis at hand.*

*In a crisis, leaders need the self-awareness to acknowledge the stresses they feel, which Ryan divides into two broad groups: threat stress and challenge stress. Threat stress is an initial sense of self-doubt often characterized by a feeling of "do I have enough knowledge, resources, skill?" Challenge stress, by contrast, is the stimulus to a winning attitude. Self-awareness provides a distance from personal stress, Ryan argues, without denying emotion. That helps avoid overcompensating and perhaps damaging performance. Say, for example, by always needing to be the smartest person in the room on every subject.*

*"If you have to hold on tight as a leader," Ryan argues, "if you have to be the expert all the time, it shows you're insecure. If you don't need to be the smartest person in the room that gives you permission to ask questions when your situation changes."*

*Which in 2020 seemed to be all the time.*

No matter the cause of a crisis, for experienced leaders patterns will emerge. In March of 2020, when the pandemic first hit, I thought it looked a lot like the Deepwater Horizon oil spill. We had shortages of resources like oil-spill containment booms and oil-removal vessels. We had to create new technologies and build a capping stack to attach to the blowout preventer. And we had to stop the flow of oil from the Macondo well. All while working at an unprecedented depth of 35,000 feet below the water's surface.

Day-to-day Deepwater Horizon was a roller coaster of threat stresses—Do we have enough? Do we know enough?—and challenge stresses, that feeling of "we have this."

In complex crises like Deepwater Horizon or COVID-19 your situation is in a perpetual state of what you can call spiral development. As new data emerges operational protocols adapt. New information comes to light, and that mandates a shift in thinking. If you have to hold on tight as a leader in a situation like that, if you have to be the expert all the time, it shows you're insecure. If you don't need to be the smartest person in the room you give yourself permission to ask questions when your situation changes.

The Coast Guard's Admiral Thad Allen was the national incident commander for Deepwater Horizon. He was not an expert in offshore drilling but he was smart enough to learn from experts. He had to do countless daily interviews, briefings and meetings. When he didn't know the answer to a question he'd say, "I don't know but I'll get your name and get right back with you." His approach engendered trust with the media but most importantly with the thousands of responders across the vast number of agencies he led. That was a lesson I learned from him. In a crisis the role of the meta-leader is to leverage the expertise of partners to create a community response. If you need people thinking you're the expert in everything you are not a meta-leader.

An incident develops into a crisis because the requirement for critical resources outpaces their availability. During COVID it was the need for PPE, ventilators, hand sanitizer, a vaccine. In some people that produced a threat stress that provoked panic. At moments like that trust in yourself is essential.

Even good leaders are susceptible to impostor syndrome in a crisis. Certainly I struggled with impostor syndrome as I moved up the ranks from junior enlisted to flag officer. I realized that it's just our response to the initial threat stress of a challenging situation. From time to time it creeps into everyone's psyche. Imposter syndrome can be a strong theme in some people's lives, particularly in women.

When I conduct one-on-one coaching I sometimes say, "Okay, you feel like you shouldn't be here, you feel you didn't deserve the promotion. If not you, then who? Who do you think should have received the promotion instead of you?" Prepared leaders shift their thoughts from the negative inner critic to the inner coach of self-confidence. It's a crucial kind of self-awareness.

Six years after Horizon I was the Ninth Coast Guard District Commander when the motor vessel *Roger Blough* grounded and remained stranded atop Gros Cap Reef in Lake Superior. The vessel straddled the international border between the United States and Canada, the bow literally in one country and the stern in another.

My Canadian counterpart and I immediately created a unified front. We exercised meta-leadership by leveraging response and salvage expertise on both sides of the border. We had a consistency of message to the media through joint press releases. We approved joint operational salvage plans. It became the international grounding no one ever heard of. To me that's success.

In any crisis it's often the people you think are strongest who surprise you most. People you thought were resilient, ready to step up, can be the ones waiting in the corner for direction from a superior. And people you thought were just hourly employees, with one eye on the door, they are the ones who can emerge with the great new ideas, creative energy and a can-do spirit.

In the Coast Guard I saw leaders at every level. I recall commanding a ship that suffered a major engine casualty. The prime-mover on a generator threw a connecting-rod. With every stroke of the piston scalding hot oil and jagged half-inch steel projectiles ripped from the engine and shot across the room. The watchstander took quick action and literally jumped on top of the running engine. He pulled the manual stops and saved the ship. He knew what to do.

For future leaders seeing new opportunities in a crisis will be prerequisite. I would not say future leaders need to be flexible. I would say they need to be *pliable*. To be flexible implies flapping in the wind, moving whichever way the wind blows. When you're pliable you recognize patterns you've seen in other crises and apply experience in a completely different way to an emerging situation.

Looking at the coronavirus response in 2020 I saw so many opportunities where meta-leadership could have been helpful. Think of how different the response could have been if it were transparent and collaborative around the globe, among scientists, among political leaders, among manufacturers.

Maybe timing was a problem. Twenty-twenty was an election year in the United States, and politics can never be ignored. They are part of your problem set, whether it's a hurricane or Deepwater Horizon. Political leadership can rally support and push operations faster. In a perfect world everyone would like to see us fight against the virus, not against each other.

In a crisis prepared leaders are opportunistic. In 2019, for example, I was consulting to a nonprofit organization. At the time there was a strong desire among employees to work from home, particularly among younger staff. The CEO and her leadership team said, "Absolutely not. We're a leadership institute, and we require face-to-face interaction." In January 2020, the client was looking for a new location because their lease was expiring and their rent was being raised. COVID hit in March, and suddenly everyone's at home. The leadership team reversed their opposition and decided to remain remote for at least a year before signing a new lease. And that decision freed up resources for new programming.

As COVID lingered my consulting practice saw an uptick in requests for training in building a resilient workforce. The first thing I'd ask executives who hired me was, "Does your workforce know what to do when they *don't* know what to do?" In the Coast Guard we refer to this kind of overarching guidance as the command watchword. Watchwords are a leadership philosophy distilled to a simple memorable phrase or two that anyone can recite. In a way they empower people to be risk managers.

In the Coast Guard my watchwords were "Honor the member, honor the mariner, honor the memory." If my crews were doing those three things they knew I had their backs. I would defend their actions to my superiors even if those actions were counter to written policies.

For example, when I was commander for the Great Lakes and Saint Lawrence Seaway one of our response boats rescued several individuals from a pleasure craft that grounded. Some of those individuals had significant injuries. With the victims on board the Coast Guard small boat the crew was proceeding as fast as possible to the closest dock to transfer them to an ambulance. They could see the ambulance driving down the road parallel to their course, making its way to the dock. Then unexpectedly the ambulance driver got out and started waving his arms. It was obvious the driver wanted the Coast Guard crew to run the small boat up on a beach and transfer the injured victims there.

Running a vessel aground in the Coast Guard leads to a full investigation, and almost always results in loss of qualifications for the coxswain and the crew. But in a split second the coxswain led his crew from the threat stress into a challenge stress. He told me later, "Ma'am, we went right down your watchword." Honor the member: Are we trained to do this? Honor the mariner: Can we transfer the injured people to the hospital sooner if we do this without taking the small boat out of service? Honor the memory: Will this have a lingering negative effect on the Coast Guard image? In a risk-management situation they knew what to do.

The following morning I was briefed on the case and informed that a formal investigation was underway. The coxswain and crew were pulled off the water pending the results. My response was that the only investigation that should be conducted was what type of recognition the crew should be given. Because that wasn't a grounding. It was a landing.

In fact, my team prepared a memo for Coast Guard Headquarters to make a recommendation to change the written policy. Researching it they learned there was a little-known provision within the Coast Guard Search and Rescue manual that allows a coxswain and crew to purposefully ground a vessel in extraordinary circumstances. Based on my watchwords the crew knew what to do even when they *didn't* know what to do.

In my opinion that's prepared leadership.

## PARAGRAPH 3

Attacking the problem and becoming solution oriented is what raises you up as a leader. Focusing only on your own motivations induces entropy instead of energizing your response in a crisis.

# Admit That You're Vulnerable

## Paul Mee

*In years to come the central lesson of the COVID era may be that pre-pared leadership requires a capacity to think about what might be called recombinant risks. Risks, in other words, that interact with other risks and mutate into something still more complex and confusingly new.*

*In that recombinant sense a cyberthreat is a lot like the coronavirus: it is innovative and it is adaptable. Yet until not long ago cyber risk was not something consistently discussed by boards of directors as a topic of leadership preparation. What changed that were the crippling impacts of major events in the five years that preceded 2020.*

*Paul Mee, a partner in Oliver Wyman's Digital and Financial Services practice, has been trained by experience to think not only about the levels of complexity created by the recombinant risks of cyberthreats but about their long tails. Specifically about their potential for arriving abruptly, as Mee puts it, "as if space aliens have landed."*

*The first thing prepared leaders need to know about cyberthreats, says Mee, is that their organizations—all organizations—are vulner-able. The successful and the resilient prepare by acknowledging this vulnerability.*

*Mee likens contemporary cyberattacks to a perfect crime. Perfect in the sense that the victim may not even know the crime has been commit-ted until it is too late. Making the threat still more complex for victims is the often-unknowable collateral damage caused by a hack. So dramatic has the degree of innovation on the bad-actor side been, says Mee, that it amounts to an invisible arms race.*

*"Organizations will be attacked," says Mee. "It's a matter of time. What can matter most may not be a matter of how stoically you defend yourself. More often it's a matter of how quickly you stand up after you trip and fall."*

*Bad actors—whether organized crime, rogue nations or political activists, sometimes in collaboration—are motivated by cybercrime's potentially handsome rewards. In 2020 ransomware attacks became big business when organizations were compelled by the coronavirus to manage their IT and its associate data exchanges on a large-scale remote basis.*

*In any crisis working with other humans is challenging. Making that harder still in 2020 was our distance from one another. As Mee points out, the seemingly overnight transition to all-remote-all-the-time frequently left us with an absence of clues to the things that make human interactions intimate and productive. Distance became an additional obstacle to the job of being sensitive to changes in the environment.*

*Twenty-twenty was a year when the important things were brought out in sharp, undeniable relief. A concern for Mee is that when the mood of emergency recedes we will revert to a more familiar posture of trusting to luck. He knows from experience how well that works out.*

In the summer of 2020 we worked with one of the largest banks on the planet to conduct a cybersecurity exercise. The way we set it up we included a hurricane and two protests and a blockade. Into those crises we introduced a progressive cyberattack. The client had never done a multivariant exercise like that with so many challenging things happening at once.

We ran it over two days. We threw them various curveballs to make it realistic. It was not a tabletop exercise involving moving pieces of paper around. This was a real as it gets without breaking something.

And unbelievably all the elements of the exercise and more erupted in the real world. Only now with the addition of wildfires. Plus third-party IT service providers subjected to targeted ransomware attacks. If I had gone to somebody a year before and said, "Prepare for attacks with these eight things happening all at the same time" they would have told me I spent too much time in one of those states where cannabis is legal.

That's where we are now. I had a computer-scientist's education. I value precision, logic and form. And in this world there is less and less precision and less predictability. We need a better ability to navigate that.

Any organization that thinks it's going to exhaustively defend itself against all cyberattacks is naive. Organizations *will* be attacked. It is simply a matter of time. It takes just one of the millions and billions of attacks to get through to create organizational damage.

A critical lesson of 2020 is that we need to better understand long-tail risks—risks we thought would never happen or that we don't consider in combination. Even a few years ago the appreciation of cyber risk as a topic was not something discussed by boards. Changing that mindset, unfortunately, needed the crippling impacts of major cyber events.

When cyberattacks happen it can be as if space aliens have landed. We don't prepare for aliens because we've never seen them before. Even when you're prepared appreciating a new risk that innovates, morphs and evolves *all the time* is incredibly hard.

When we had the WannaCry ransomware attack in 2017 there were hospitals that were on pencil and paper for months before they came back online. Norsk Hydro was stymied for months. They scrambled to buy fax machines on eBay or wherever they could to be able to restore the most basic and critical communications. Or go back to 2014 and the Home Depot hacks. Hackers got in through the heating-and-ventilation controls, and from there jumped to the payment system.

Home Depot was one of the early adopters of cyber insurance. Their original cyber-insurance coverage was in the tens of millions. As of December 2019 the cost of their cyber incident ran into several hundred million dollars.

We have gotten better. There has not been a WannaCry cyber crisis equivalent for a few years now. That does not mean there's not going to be. Cyberattacks or a data breach remain hard to fully understand at a given point in time. They change rapidly. Increasingly we're seeing the concept of sustained systems attacks, whereby a government entity or *Fortune* 1000 organization is subject to persistent targeted attacks. These cyber campaigns by rogue actors constantly probe for pathways into what are often our most important enterprises for services, power and health.

During 2020 we saw a massive uptick in ransomware. The bad actors realized that a lot of the digital systems upon which we are reliant had become critical because physical premises were typically not accessible due to the pandemic. Financial services, utilities, electronic communications, telemedicine—if criminals locked users out services like that are likely to pay up. With victims compelled to pay we have seen ransomware demands go from hundreds of thousands of dollars to tens of millions. The bad actors are well motivated, highly innovative, and, annoyingly, unlikely to get caught and punished.

More worrying is that the type of individual who conducts a cyberattack typically does not understand the consequences. In the military there is a strategic consideration when conducting an attack. You know there will be ramifications. You are prepared for retaliation; you understand what the collateral damage could be. But an amateur or an activist who wants to make a difference, or a criminal who wants to extort money, does not necessarily appreciate or care about collateral damage. That makes cyber risk both unpredictable in terms of when it will happen and in terms of its scale of impact when it *does* happen.

The degree of innovation on the bad-actor side is incredible. It is an invisible arms race. Organized crime connects with activists and with hackers on the dark web or by other means. Rogue nations readily acquire capabilities on a highly attractive economic basis. The open-source nature of the dark web and bad-actor communities puts anti-antivirus capabilities and other dangerous cyberattack weaponry in the hands of those with potentially the lowest moral standards and the highest motivation to create chaos.

Not long ago I worked with one client whose attackers decided to find information about all the executive assistants in the client's organization. They realized that an executive assistant probably has as much access to sensitive information as the executive they support. Most organizations would not immediately consider the threat to staff in the support orbit of an executive. You need to quickly respond to those idiosyncratic situations by thinking like a determined hacker. Be in a position to take the lesson from one situation to other situations as quickly as possible.

There are more subtle occasions when a nation is conducting espionage. They may want to steal your IP. They may want to steal information about your executives, whether it's their personal circumstances or, potentially, that of their families. Rogue actors may simply want to observe and learn how you respond when a cyber rock is thrown through your organizational pane of glass. Without sufficient diligence these can be hard to see.

Cyber is the modern manifestation of the perfect crime. If someone steals your jewelry you know it's gone. With a cybercrime they may just make a copy of your data and you may not even know it has happened until after a protracted period of information siphoning. That was what we saw with the Panama Papers.

We have had to get smarter at looking for unusual behaviors. We have seen the application of artificial intelligence and machine-based learning to the way people use their computers, how they look at data. We try to spot the perfect crime by looking for clues and fingerprints in digital signals.

Hackers are doing things to corrupt systems beyond what you might read in the newspaper. In the Middle East there was an attempt to compromise Bitcoin. The way they did it was to buy Bitcoin and put a tag in it, a tiny link to pornography. The ambition was to render Bitcoin as something that could not be used by certain communities or in certain jurisdictions.[17]

The good thing is we're learning and building muscle memory for these kinds of events. We're building more resilient and recoverable infrastructure systems and capabilities. There is increasingly less "it'll never happen to us" thinking. Everybody can be and, at some

---

[17] "The Flaw that May Bring Down Bitcoin or Change it Forever." *Global Guerrillas.* April 20, 2013.

stage likely will be, compromised. But when it happens we will know better what to do.

Defensive technology will only take you so far. You need to get human beings involved. Navigating events that are new in our experience requires learning from previous situations. As human beings we have an amazing capacity to innovate and learn. But we need to make the time to synthesize.

The nature of a cyberthreat is a lot like the coronavirus: it's innovative, it's adaptable, it's unpredictable. With the coronavirus we are at a point whereby the threat is a finite thing—for now. We will learn how to neutralize it or vaccinate it. We can hope to learn from *this* coronavirus how to deal with the *next* coronavirus. If we don't we risk being structurally in a constant stop/start motion at personal, organizational and nationwide levels.

We are unlikely to be as fortunate when it comes to cyberattacks. The next major successful cyberattack will not look like previous attacks. That is what makes us vulnerable.

Quantum computing is coming on fast as a commercially viable capability. Quantum computers will be able to solve problems that are far too complex for classical computers to figure out. This includes solving the algorithms behind encryption keys that protect our data and the integrity of the Internet. Quantum could create incredible vulnerability. It will be the nuclear power of the next digital generation. We need safeguards and rules.

It's probably counter to how Western human beings think about leadership but we need to embrace vulnerability. There are a lot of times, especially in a challenging situation, when you need to put yourself in a vulnerable position. You will need the fortitude to deal with it. Because you may be doing so on behalf of many other people.

For instance, it occurred to me that if the citizens of a nation were literate with respect to cyber and cyber threats then that nation would likely have less cyber-risk exposure. So I got sponsorship from my firm to conduct research into cyber-risk literacy by geography.[18] We produced an index of countries ranking cyber-risk literacy based on a score out of 1,000. Given the criticality of the human element it was essential to calibrate and communicate this ranking without bias.

Education is the chief marker of cyber literacy. Israel, for example, has a proclivity to care about national security. It has the highest number of cyber-related businesses per capita in the world. Its education system considers the potential cyber literacy of children as young as eight years old. At a later age cyber literacy influences what an individual citizen will do during their national service.

So consider my personal vulnerability here. Countries not ranked in the top five will be unhappy. They will challenge me. I had to make sure I had what I needed in terms of logic, practicalities and perception. I assembled experts on education, government policy and cyber risk as the Index Governance Committee. They check on me and check on the index. They check on its logic, check on its source data. They challenge me to translate vulnerabilities into risk-management strategies.

That's an example of what I mean by admitting your vulnerability. Another example is being willing to lead people who are smarter than you are.

Probably 30 years ago I was the youngest manager of my grade for a new venture being sponsored by a major UK bank. I was told to go build a team. That was a new experience. In my previous roles the team was in place and I had been either inserted or promoted. I asked what kind of people I should hire. My boss at the time said, "Hire people you consider smarter than you and at least as driven."

You might think, well, if I do that they're going to take my job, they're going to be a threat. If you think that way you won't get the best. Look for people who make you say, "I want this person on my team because they are supersmart, they're going to be motivated, they're going to be as passionate as I am."

---

[18] Cyber Risk Literacy and Education Index. Mee, Brandenburg & Lin. Oliver Wyman Forum. October 2020.

One of the worst leadership traits you can have is the hubris to think you need to have all the answers. Unwarranted self-confidence can blind you to the benefits of having expertise surround you. Mix excessive self-confidence with somebody in a position of authority and a lot of damage can be done. You need a culture where people feel sufficient trust to embrace a degree of vulnerability and say, "I don't know."

In 2020 we got some strong insights regarding the ways we operate as human beings—how we manage, how we work together in our professional lives. For instance, one year I recall traveling a quarter of a million miles to visit people because I believed that was the principal and only effective means of communicating and persuading, especially in sensitive personal-advisory situations. In 2020 we learned quickly that interaction by digital means can often be sufficient. We also learned our work lives don't have to involve spending hours commuting or days traveling at the expense of time with family and community. We also bumped into the limits of our relationship with technology.

At the height of the crisis a colleague of mine, Keith McCambridge, did a webinar with me regarding workforce fortitude and the COVID lockdown. I was the practical guy saying this is how you make sure data does not get stolen, here's what to do about securing your computer, here's what to do in a drastic situation or a cyber crisis. As a professional psychologist Keith talked about the impact of the lockdown on us as human beings, the challenges to our mental work template, and the fatigue associated with being in isolated situations where the environment doesn't change even if the videoconference topic does.

Keith argued that, as human beings, we have evolved to use context for clues about the roles we play, how to behave, even the intonation of our speech. A CEO, for example, will take a quite different posture on stage with shareholders than at home with our children

We use the clues around us to become a different person. In one environment I am the cyber executive, in another I'm the manager or coach, in another I'm the father, in another I'm the student. There used to be time to prepare before crossing lines—an airplane journey, a train ride, even a two-minute elevator ride. Consider how many times a team of yours has assembled in the lobby of a client's building to collectively get into the game.

If we are in video conferences from morning until late we are typically in the same physical environment with none of the familiar clues about what's next and the role we should be adopting. It is exhausting. While there are productivity gains avoiding Zoom fatigue is becoming a new skill.

Twenty years ago during my annual review my then boss commented that "some people work well under pressure. You work *best* under pressure." It's why I often work at the edge on projects requiring the navigation of obscurity and risk. It's a useful trait for getting stuff done. But there are downsides. Many important, often critical, issues are not direct and tangible. They might not be immediately life-threatening but they matter a lot.

Politics aside, I think this is why we have dragged our feet and not been collectively committed to climate resilience. It has not felt truly urgent to us individually and to those in power. Our collective endeavors to creating a vaccine in an incredibly short period of time are amazing, a testament to what we can do when a crisis is real and present. As for our climate, 2020 was the strongest message yet regarding a phenomenon for which we are all fundamentally vulnerable and on which we collectively need to act.

# Adapt and Overcome

## Command Sergeant Major
## Michael Hall (Ret.)

*Someone once described Command Sergeant Major Michael Hall (Ret.) as "an out of the box thinker who understands what the box really is." And in 2020 Mike Hall found too many organizations in a box full of wishful thinking.*

*General Stanley McChrystal, interviewed elsewhere in this book, once described Hall as "the best soldier I have ever known." He is a decorated combat veteran with over 34 years of service to the US Army Special Operations, including 20 years with the 75th Ranger Regiment. He has been the senior advisor to seven general officers in war and peace.*

*Hall retired from active duty in 2008 with the rank of command sergeant major, the Army's highest enlisted rank. He was almost immediately recalled in 2009 to serve as Senior Enlisted Advisor for the International Security Assistance Force North Atlantic Treaty Organization, Afghanistan/United States Forces Afghanistan. The force comprised over 130,000 soldiers from 46 countries during the most dramatic change in strategy in the history of the war.*

*After his second retirement from the Army Hall brought his experience to the private sector, including Lockheed Martin and Scotts Miracle Gro, where he was chief of staff for North American Sales. He has been a coach to senior executives at a diverse collection of companies, working to focus them on improving culture, communication, strategic planning and operational effectiveness.*

*Experience has persuaded Hall that most of us are slow to recognize transformative moments. We're even slower to realize that after such crises the world never goes back to the way it was—and that's not always a bad thing. Hall views the COVID-19 virus as a historic changemaker on a par with world wars and plagues, the kind of event that alters us for good. It stands to reason that it should do the same for our organizations.*

*Even before a crisis hits, Hall insists, leaders should be treating their organizations as burning platforms. By that he means looking to a future we can't predict but which we know will be different—in some cases radically different—from the one for which the organizations were built.*

*There are risks on a burning platform, as Hall is the first to admit. For a start, why look beyond what has—until now—been working well? Why trade the comfort of the familiar for the near-term costs of pursuing something at which we might fail, at least at first? No wonder organizations resist, even in a worldwide crisis.*

*It is in moments of crisis that leaders are called upon to take risks and defend them with a credible vision. That's not cheerleading. It can mean the transparent acknowledgement of pain. For Hall that's how leaders model accountability. And not wishful thinking.*

*Hall's ideas about transforming organizations in response to crisis is tempered by a conviction that "people don't change." What can be changed, he argues, is environment. And environments change behavior.*

*Organizations are powerfully prone to habit—especially if they've had success. Changing them takes patience. For leaders and subordinates, Hall suggests, the rewards of being clear-eyed in a crisis can be exhilarating.*

When the Afghan war started, John Mulholland and his organization were up north and our organization was down south. We were both in war-fighting units. We would ask for things and sometimes we'd get some weird responses. It was always a response that would make me want to say, "Listen, you may think this war is going to be over in six months but it isn't. It's going to go on for a long time. We're going to be here for a while."

That's the kind of box we're in now. It's a box full of wishful thinking.

People wanted to believe in 2020 that, 18 months later, we would have COVID figured out and we would go back to what we were doing in 2019. They want to picture full baseball stadiums. But we are never going back. Our training pipelines, our recruiting pipelines, our retention pipelines—they all need to adjust to a new reality. Organizations need to figure out what they want to look like after the immediate crisis and then find people who can deliver that vision.

Big change in the world comes from big events like wars or religious revolutions or a plague. Those affect everything, from industry to education. The world of 1939 was not the world of 1945. The world after the pandemic five years from now will be changed just as significantly. Even after we beat the virus the world will be different.

Already the way the rest of the world looks at America is significantly different. A lot of people will say it was Trump. It was COVID.

Most organizations are good at figuring out what they want to look like tomorrow. A great organization tries to figure out what they're going to look like the day *after* tomorrow. To me that's the difference between managing and leading.

Even before a crisis hits leadership should be treating their organization like a burning platform. But how do you train men and women to thrive on a burning platform?

Right now what most of us have is a recruiting system driven by requirements that are almost always out of date. People advance based on performance, not potential. They get to where they are by doing what they did. The Army is famous for this. And I guarantee you 99 percent of larger organizations have the same problem.

There is risk in recruiting someone based on potential. At the end of the day you have still got to make your quarterly numbers. That's a leadership responsibility. Leaders decide what organizational risks to accept.

Eventually the environment is going to catch up to you. How many of the *Fortune* 500 companies from fifty years ago are still in business? About 10 percent. They got bigger but they didn't get better. If you don't build in flexibility you'll be irrelevant quick.

I'll give you an example.

When I was with the Ranger regiment we were exceptionally good at what we did. And still we needed a significant shakeup. The kind of leaders we had, the kind of thinking we were comfortable with had to go. We treated everything as a burning platform.

We had the opportunity, for instance, to get night-vision devices to outfit the entire regiment. We put them on people's faces and told them they couldn't take them off. They were going to learn how to fight with night-vision devices.

At first it was terrible. We prided ourselves on being able to see in the dark for 200 yards. That's how we're all raised. It was a significant change that carried significant risk. Our marksmanship standards went from among the best in the Army to mediocre because we were learning new equipment. People who used to know how to teach people to shoot didn't know how to teach people to embrace this new technology.

Some leaders didn't adapt. So we started hiring different kinds of people who didn't fit the traditional mold. We looked for people who hadn't been inculcated with the old ways of doing business. Sometimes you need to slow down if you want to go fast.

The same thing happened when I was with Scotts. It was the industry leader in lawn-and-garden supplies. They were so big that competitors would say, "Well, we can't take on Scotts. But we can take on rodent control or we can get a little bit of the grass-seed business." They chipped away and chipped away. Scotts was still making a lot of money. Why invent a new grass seed when you've already got 59 percent of the market? But it wasn't going to be long before all those little chips amounted to something. So we changed the culture to be much more aggressive, much more innovative.

I don't believe you can change people. We're all products of our experiences. But you *can* change how people behave by changing the environment you put them in. That's how you change organizations.

Most military organizations are not like that. Most commercial organizations aren't either. It's like the marksmanship example I gave you. Too many leaders don't have the patience and don't want to take the risk. Leadership has to truly underwrite the risk.

If leaders want their organizations to innovate and grow in a post-crisis environment they've got to spend time on the things that make them uncomfortable. That's their personal burning platform.

The Army's emphasis on after-action reviews was a brilliant idea. We'd sit down and get everybody to be brutally honest about what went wrong and what needed to get better. Everybody had an equal voice. It revealed future leaders, the people who were not afraid to make the organization better. You either adapted to that environment or you went somewhere else.

We learn from mistakes. But there are better ways to teach people. Leaders need to make sure people don't make mistakes that are preventable. That's defining risk acceptance. How do you make someone understand what is acceptable risk and what isn't? You take the time to define what success is.

We talk about metrics all the time. Usually we have a hard time figuring out what those metrics are. It's easy if it's a number, if it's a time—you know, for report cards. But most metrics are harder to define than that. You improve people's understanding of acceptable risk by spending time defining success. In the Army it's what we called commander's guidance.

Most senior leaders are good at defining what success is for *them*. They usually got hired because they had a vision. But they don't take the time to define what success is for, say, marketing, so that marketing understands what its risks are and how far it should go. And when it needs to ask for help. And most importantly, when to stand up and say, "This isn't going to work." Too many organizations are afraid of that. They keep throwing good money away.

Senior leaders understand this when I'm doing coaching work. Their problem is communicating it down two and three levels. True intent gets lost.

Organizations generally do not do a good job building communication systems that incentivize lower-level feedback—informing *up*, I call it. People at the top feel threatened by that. They think, "Wait a minute, I got where I am based on what I know and on my previous performance. *Now* you're introducing something I had nothing to do with?"

In a crisis senior leaders need to directly communicate at least two levels down. They need to set priorities and enforce them. They need to model personal accountability. Do those things and the chances of being understood the way the leader wants to be understood are pretty good. It makes leaders at every level much more effective.

Responding to crisis can't be about doing more with less. Especially in emergencies nobody has any whitespace on their calendars. Just telling people to work harder lasts about a week before everyone falls back into the same old thing. In response to a stressful new directive subordinates are usually thinking, Alright, tell me what you want me to *stop* doing. That's the tactical part of decision making, the things that we're going to either ramp down over time or we're just going to stop doing as we adapt to the new environment.

I think most people *want* to live on a burning platform. Good people like excitement in their life. If you tell them what they're going to do and what they are not going to do, life is less exhausting without all the fire drills. It's a very steady rhythm if it's done right. You know what you're doing, you know where you're going. You're not getting interrupted because someone is yelling, "Here's the issue of the day. Everyone stop what you're doing!" *That's* what exhausts people.

In the summer of 2020 I saw this awesome dude walking through the Atlanta airport in a full hazmat suit. He had goggles on and a hood and everything. The ironic thing was that no one stopped and stared. They were sort of, sure, okay. Imagine that guy walking through an airport in a hazmat suit six months before.

It was a small example of people learning to accept significant change. It was also an early indicator of our new normal.

# You Can't Rush A Crisis

## Lawrence M. "Larry" Drake II, PhD

*By 2013 Larry Drake had already worked around the world in senior roles for large organizations like The Coca-Cola Company, Cablevision Systems Corporation, Kraft Foods and PepsiCo. He advised technology startups and along the way picked up both a PhD in psychology and an MBA. All these experiences, he contends, the good and the bad, were preparation for crises both personal and professional, crises of the sort that try character and faith.*

*Twenty-thirteen was the year Drake was asked to take on the role of President and CEO of LEAD, a program for high-potential minority students with an interest in professional business careers. His role at LEAD regularly causes Drake to reflect on the nature of prepared leadership.*

*"Everything we do in life prepares us for the next thing," Drake insists. "Everything has meaning, everything has value, even if it doesn't turn out the way we want."*

*Drake, like several others interviewed for this book, is a believer in battle drills, in thinking through what might happen and how to respond, especially in the worst case. The objective of battle drills is not to predict crises and how they will play out. The objective is to prepare the mind to be alert to a new kind of challenge when it makes its appearance. Otherwise there is a risk of forcing analogies to past experience when the problem before us is wholly new.*

*"You train your mind," Drake says, "for an alertness that tells you 'This moment is different. This is not like that.'"*

*In crisis moments, acting reflexively can be fatal to a good decision. As Drake puts it, "You can't rush a crisis." Remembering this requires high self-awareness, a concept Drake argues is not a measure of how we think about ourselves but of how we understand the effect we have on other people.*

*For Drake, the brutal experience of standing by his daughter in her ultimately unsuccessful fight with cancer in 2017 offered a hard example of how even the right choices may still bring grief. That grief and ultimate celebration of his daughter's life is described in Drake's 2017 book* Color Him Father.[19]

*The coronavirus that infected the world in 2020 and the social upheaval that accompanied it in the United States offered opportunities to think fresh thoughts and to imagine a world better than it was. For Drake, "Those twin disruptions exposed what happens when leaders can't or won't meet the moment."*

One morning when I was CEO of Coca-Cola West Africa I got a call at two a.m. My chief security guy told me that a hundred of my employees had been kidnapped for ransom. One of the decisions I had to make within the first 30 minutes was whether to notify the US embassy. I was sure that if I did they would categorize it as a terrorist situation.

This was six hours ahead of the news cycle in the United States. I couldn't afford to have the outcome be a share-price decline or a public flogging of our company as a result of having a kidnapping characterized as a terrorist act. If it were we would lose any leverage we had. Our priority was to get those people released without a ransom, which we weren't going to pay because of the Foreign Corrupt Practices Act. Knowing there were a hundred lives at stake I made the decision not to tell the embassy. We got those people out in less than six hours. We paid no ransom. A lot of people collaborated to make it happen.

You need to meet the moment in a crisis. And in 2020 we had two crises. We had COVID-19. And we had an unstable social consciousness, one of the most unstable in our history. Those twin dis-

---

[19] *Color Him Father*. Lawrence M. Drake II. Brown Girls Books. 2017.

ruptions exposed what happens when leaders can't or won't meet the moment.

In a crisis the clock may be ticking but you still have to take the time to think through where you'll end up. When you don't have the benefit of time you have to be methodical. You have to think through the impact of your decisions on the people who will carry them out. You have to think through to the other side of your crisis.

Here's an analogy. If you have ever been divorced you know you have to think about more than your immediate situation. You may be done with your spouse but you're never done with your kids. You have to ensure that your kids not only survive but thrive on the other side of the crisis, when *they* become parents. It's the same with behaviors you model for the people you're leading.

I am president of an organization called LEAD, which stands for LEADership, Education and Development. It started in 1980 when The Wharton School at the University of Pennsylvania part-nered with several corporations in and around Philadelphia and New York to create a pipeline of high-potential minority students. Since our beginnings over 21,000 students have completed our pro-gram—99.8 percent of them graduating from college, most in four years. They include people like Raphael Bostic, the president of the Atlanta Federal Reserve, and Luis Ubinas, the former president of the Ford Foundation.

At LEAD we talk about leadership in terms of preparation. We talk about listening skills, the ability to collaborate, the ability to dis-agree and still be able to move forward. Our kids learn to deal with uncertainty.

Periodically, I go to campuses for what we call a fireside chat. I talk about the uncertainties they are going to face. And I ask ques-tions. The first is, what are you most afraid of? Because fear is an engine that can drive you to dangerous places. They'll answer with things like, "I'm afraid to die" or "I'm afraid I'm not going to measure up to my expectations or the expectations of the people who have supported me." All kinds of things come out of their mouths. Then I ask, how much time do you spend thinking about what you're afraid of? And these kids spend just an enormous amount of time in their fears. Ask them how many times they talk to their parents about what they are afraid of and the answer is usually zero.

I come from what others would describe as meager beginnings. That's not a new story. We lost a couple of our houses. At one point we were sleeping in the hallway of a building not far from a place from which we had been kicked out. I had no interest in going to college. I just wanted a job, and I did not want to do anything to disgrace my family.

When I talk to my young LEAD scholars about critical thinking and problem solving, I share some of the childhood crisis stories, including when I was homeless as a teenager. Occupying those cold wooden steps with the wind whistling through every crevice I had critical decisions to make about what I would do if somebody walked in the door and wanted to rob or harm me. It was some of the best critical thinking I've ever done. What was true then, and still is today, is that you have to be able to think things through by considering various scenarios even when you don't have a lot of time to do it.

Everything we do in life prepares us for the next thing. Everything has meaning, everything has value, even if it does not turn out the way we want.

More recently, I think about the process of my daughter's treatment during the last eight months of her life. There were decisions she and I and her mom had to make about what kind of treatment to take on. What were the potential outcomes, good or not? We made decisions that were the best we could hope to make. It did not turn out the way we hoped but that didn't mean we made bad decisions. We tried so hard to think it through during the biggest crisis of my daughter's life and ours.

Even before that, when my daughter's condition began to worsen, her doctors wanted to put her on a lung-transplant list. The average life expectancy of someone who has a lung transplant is six years. And my daughter said, "Six years is really putting me in a box. I think I have a better chance of living longer by taking even better care of myself." She made the argument in the midst of her own personal crisis and that of her family. We believed that was the right decision. More important, *she* believed it.

I am blessed to work with my wife in our business called HOPE 360 INC, which stands for Helping Other People Excel. We do this through leadership development, organization effectiveness and executive coaching. In the coaching work I do with senior executives one of the questions I often ask is, "What makes you cry?" Most of these folks are men, so you can imagine the response. Some say things like, "When my daughter falls and I see her cry I get emotional. I can't stand to see my daughter hurt." Some can't even do that. They have ignored their fears for so long. What happens as a consequence is that they are usually the least self-aware people in the world.

Self-awareness plays a huge role in dealing with crisis and decision-making. It is not just about how aware you are of yourself but of how aware you are of the impact you have on other people. People who do not have a high degree of self-awareness generally are not aware of those around them. That gets noticed by the people they lead. It can create consequences that in a crisis work against them. It's toxic.

As an executive coach I use something akin to Joseph Campbell's work on the hero's journey. Campbell points out that every hero eventually meets a foe who is not defeated by the hero's superpower. That requires the hero to swiftly come up with a new plan to defeat that enemy. It is the moment of tension that creates a new solution to a problem. That's how innovation happens. The trick is to constantly challenge ourselves to expand our portfolio of solutions. If I said I did this 100 percent of the time I would be lying.

I don't see a lot of companies built for crisis management. They sort of repeat themselves according to their comfort zone. If a solution to a problem worked once they respond that way every time even if the problems really are not the same. No matter what happens they say, "Yeah, looks familiar." We need to deal with each crisis as it presents itself, not as we would like it to be.

Many times I have asked my managers, okay, say I give you the resources to do what you say you want to do. What are you going to do if what you want does not happen? In my experience, many organizations don't take the time to figure that out.

I got my PhD in Psychology so I could understand how people think and gain insight into how they behave. We can learn just as much or more from a bad leader as we can from a good one. All those things prepare us. You can't cherry-pick only what's good. Leaders are shaped by both buckets of learning.

I once worked for PepsiCo, running a billion-dollar division in their restaurant group. Part of my responsibility included the KFC business in Chicagoland with over 1,200 restaurants and 6,000 employees. One day a senior executive came to visit me. We went down to the South Side of Chicago, down near the old Comiskey Park. Our brand-new restaurant stood right across the street from Cabrini Green, one of the largest housing projects at that time. It was on pace to deliver a million dollars in sales annually.

During surprise store visits we focused on curb appeal, customer service and food preparation. After a thorough review the senior exec and I agreed the store wasn't up to scratch. The grass had not been cut the way it should have been, and the lawn stood out like a sore thumb. We talked to the restaurant GM and to my director of operations, who was also onsite. We agreed we would come back the next day to see if there was improvement.

When we showed up the inside was better but the outside looked the way it had the day before. The people they called to cut the grass never showed up, which in that part of Chicago was nothing to be surprised about. Not wanting to discuss this inside the unit we moved to the parking lot. I spoke to the store manager, and the senior executive was in earshot. He came over to me with members of my leadership team standing close by. Most of those in this parking lot were Black, as was most of my leadership team. Much to my surprise the senior exec looked at me and he said, "You can't seem to get your people to get things done. Didn't I say yesterday I wanted this place to be better condition today? Get your ass down there and pick those weeds up that you can't seem to get taken care of."

Now I have got a second to decide whether I am going to pick up those weeds or whether I am going to exercise the rage I feel and physically retaliate. Some members of my team lurched toward me as if they wanted to do it for me. They were embarrassed for me, the

Black man in charge. I waved them off. I decided I would pick up the weeds.

It did not diminish my dignity. That was the lesson for my team. And I knew what they thought of this senior leader. I would discuss it with many of them later. It was clear his behavior that day made them not want to work for a company that had people like him, a White guy standing in the middle of a Black neighborhood, acting like that.

When we got back in the car I couldn't take it anymore because I was so angry. I looked over at him and said, "If you ever embarrass me like that again…" He eventually reassigned me to corporate headquarters.

Several months later, while working at headquarters, I saw him. After catching his eye I said, "Hey, can we get together and talk sometime?" He said sure, maybe you can join my wife and me for dinner. It shocked me. Blew me away might be a better description. Several weeks later I arrived at his home and during the evening we talked about the business and about everything but the incident that occurred that hot summer morning in Chicago. After his wife left the table I said to him, "Thank you." He thought I meant for dinner. I said I enjoyed dinner but my thank you was for the incident with the weeds. Because that day was a moment that taught me things I would not otherwise have learned. He was floored.

I must tell you, stories like that are not abnormal in the life of a Black leader. Black people in this country are enraged a lot of the time. In the end we all know we can't let it get the better of us. Sometimes it does. You have to find the will to focus on the prize. To be able to raise your children, to be able to work, you have to be able to accomplish things. You can't allow the bad behavior of others to bring you down or rob you of your dreams.

Examples of systemic racism in this country and how it targets me or my family create crisis moments almost every day of my life. In an instant I often have to say to myself, "What I did last time with one person may not work with this person, in this situation." You need to be careful not to outsmart yourself. Often there are simple solutions. Other times the situation is more complex than what you think you see.

To be sure, every event that is problematic or uncomfortable is not necessarily a crisis. But when crisis comes we can't rush through it even though it requires quick action. I know that's a paradox. But how leaders and people respond to moments of crisis and its disruptive force is more important than the crisis itself.

# How To Think About Your Worst Day

## Lieutenant General Mary A. Legere (Retired)

*In July 2012 Mary Legere was a panelist at the Aspen Ideas Festival in Colorado. She was asked to describe the future of military intelligence. "Fusion," she said. The ability to move quickly through data, to see through layers of multidiscipline intelligence and find meaning in context, and to communicate that to decision makers.*

*When Legere made those comments she was a newly promoted Lieutenant General and the Army's Deputy Chief of Staff for Intelligence. She was responsible for the readiness, operations and modernization of the Army's 58,000-person Military Intelligence Corps. She was selected for the position after nearly three decades in a succession of increasingly complex leadership and intelligence positions around the world, including service as the Commanding General of the Army's 17,000-person Intelligence and Security Command. She was the Senior Military Intelligence Officer supporting Multi-National Force Iraq and the United States Forces in Korea and Combined Forces Command. In her military career Legere commanded and supported intelligence forces in over 120 countries including Germany, Bosnia, Iraq and the Republic of Korea. She was just the fourth woman in the US Army's 237-year history to achieve the rank of Lieutenant General.*

*After four years as the Army's Senior Intelligence Officer Legere retired and in 2016 joined Accenture Federal Services as a Managing*

*Director leading its National and Defense Intelligence practice. She chairs the National Military Intelligence Foundation, a nonprofit for students and professionals aspiring to intelligence and national-security work. She also serves on advisory boards in support of the US intelligence community.*

*It is remarkable how much of Legere's conversation about prepared leadership centers on developing people to thrive amid volatility.*

*"If you assume change is constant," Legere argues, "it is essential then for leaders to be comfortable viewing disruption as both an opportunity and risk. Leaders should inspire their organizations to embrace innovation. The approaches they have grown comfortable may be obsolete."*

*As much as leaders would like to know with certainty the consequences of change they must prepare teams to rehearse responses to the full range of options that could disrupt them—a variant of the battle drills practiced by other interviewees in this book. The purpose of these rehearsals is to make a reflex of disciplined, practiced approaches to change.*

*And never forget, says Legere, that your future, like your enemy, has a vote.*

All my life I've benefited from mentors who modeled behaviors that contributed to my development. One of the most memorable was an instructor who offered a perspective on the importance of accepting change as a constant. I remember running into him with a few of my classmates at the end of a long training day. We were in the final weeks of an intelligence officer basic course, and he offered some sage advice. He said if we wanted to succeed in taking care of our soldiers and our missions when we arrived at our units we needed to be prepared to adapt, to accept and embrace change—in other words, to be comfortable with being uncomfortable.

I remember specifically the way he pointed out that everything we spent months learning about the enemy, about technology and about tradecraft would be in constant flux. It needed to be if it was going to remain relevant. He told us to seek the hardest jobs, learn constantly and train our unit to do the same.

In the next 30 years I thought about that encounter a lot. Particularly when I met leaders transfixed by the present, whose units

146

were competent but too comfortable. Leaders who spent too little time challenging themselves to think about the future and its risks.

Whenever I encountered organizations whose leaders embraced change as a constant—who instilled what you might call a cultural bias for continuous improvement—I knew those were organizations I wanted to be part of. They had leaders I wanted to emulate. I just needed experience putting their ideas in practice.

Let me tell you about the most formative experience in my development as a leader.

Just as I was completing my twelfth year in the military I was a newly promoted Army major and a recent graduate of the Army's Command and General Staff College. At the time I was making the shift from leading successfully at the tactical- and smaller-unit level to preparing to lead larger organizations and intelligence enterprises at the operational and strategic levels. It was a inflection point in my career. I knew I needed to learn how to drive innovation and change at a regional and, eventually, a global scale.

To accelerate my development, I requested a two-year assignment to the Military Intelligence Brigade in the Republic of Korea. The brigade was responsible for providing intelligence and early warning to the over 700,000 Korean and US ground forces that defend the Republic of Korea from North Korean aggression. I'd served there previously. I knew the operational environment would be fast-paced and require all I had as a professional. I was looking forward to working extremely hard and growing in the process.

I had also done my homework on the brigade's new commander. I knew he was regarded as one of Army Intelligence Corps' most forward-thinking leaders. He was a combat leader who demanded the highest standards of himself and his subordinates. Be prepared, one of his admirers told me, to work harder than you ever have in your life.

I always enjoyed the stress of continuous adaptation. But I often struggled to know if I was bringing others along. I could not have picked a more brilliant—or tougher—teacher. He worked with leaders outside and across the organization to set strategy and priorities for his 24-month command. Because at some point almost every major joint, coalition, multinational and interagency partner is part of the theater's war plans.

As an experienced combat commander he knew the brigade was already highly proficient and creative in executing its 24/7 intelligence tasks in support of daily operations. He was determined to expand its readiness for wartime missions. He was thinking in advance about replicating the difficulty and the levels of interconnectedness that would be required on our worst day—say, if war were to erupt on the Korean peninsula.

To ensure buy-in at every level the commander instituted a holistic leader-development program to train leaders on the rationale for our efforts. It tied them to their responsibility for contributing to improving the brigade's ability to meet its armistice and wartime obligations.

The brigade commander led from the center. As part of every newcomer and leader development program he led discussions on thinking about change. He conveyed his urgency to every member of our unit. He was not just soliciting support but tapping pockets of resistance that might need to be reengaged.

Preparing yourself and your organization for war is certainly a requirement of all military leaders. My commander took this urgency to the next level. He required each team to think deeply about what was needed to drive improvement and to create and then deliver a complex series of exercises that taken together significantly improve the brigade's ability to prevail.

Quarter after quarter, in addition to meeting its daily mission requirements our units tested and validated new approaches through multiunit exercises. These were rehearsals for unprecedented risk. The operational rigor created significant stress on what was already a demanding mission environment. But I was excited to see how relentless the commander worked to educate, to enlist allies and reduce resistance. It changed the culture of the organization. It resulted in new approaches that increased the readiness not only of the brigade but of the dozens of organizations and warfighting staffs that joined us.

I was a student of this process. And I noticed that an important element in collective ownership was getting subordinate commanders and officers to work together in attacking seemingly intractable readiness problems. Maybe that meant exploring new relationships with organizations that might be vital to our mission performance in war or a crisis. We built teams across the organization to improve specific aspects of our missions. That compelled everyone in the organization to contribute to a unified intention.

For two intense years my colleagues and I had a daily dose of leader development. Leaders at every level, including support elements, were engaged in experimentation and process improvement. The commander took time to guide and celebrate the efforts of people—intelligence professionals, aviators, support staffs, linguists, supply and maintenance personnel, chaplains, legal advisors. Everyone. He did it whether we were driving the program to increase intelligence interoperability with our Korean counterparts, or expanding the synergies between our Aviation organization and the Air and Maritime component commands, or increasing the readiness of maintainers, analysts, engineers or cooks.

The commander insisted that rank did not equal brains. Often the game changers were contributions coming from engaged junior soldiers and civilians who were part of our brigade or another supporting organization. They provided paths to solutions that otherwise might not have been forthcoming.

In an intelligence organization we are often reminded that the future, like the enemy, has a vote. That informed the way we rehearsed risks, opportunities and worst-case eventualities that might disrupt a plan. The part of this process I appreciated most then and for the rest of my professional life was the commander's disciplined approach to wargaming and rehearsals. When the concept for even a routine exercise was briefed to the commander and his staff planners would be challenged to name what might defeat or disrupt their plan. Should those conditions begin to materialize, he'd ask, what are the indicators of disruption? What risks or opportunities will you proactively rehearse to ensure that you can still achieve your mission? The intention was not to discourage innovation or unproven approaches. It was to increase opportunities for success by assuring ourselves that we had thought through contingencies. That forced us to move beyond what we thought would happen to anticipate what could go wrong.

Disciplined wargaming against potential disruption was particularly important as we increased the complexity of our operations. We became accustomed to thinking in multiple time dimensions, to thinking critically about the details that underpin innovation. Over time we brought new clarity to crisis action planning. With practice we evolved into an organization of leaders with the discipline to envision and exploit disruption. If the situation required it we could decisively regroup and retain momentum.

I'm telling you this story because my experience in Korea was invaluable as I progressed through my career. I was able to see how an inspired leader could drive an organization content with being able to execute its assigned tasks to become a dynamic learning organization, one whose members were invested in pushing the limits of innovation.

In Korea I saw how leaders set the conditions that support continuous improvement. For me it confirmed the role of leaders in educating their organizations to remain abreast of emerging threats. In a crisis a prepared leader can create a culture that encourages disciplined experimentation and agile responses. That includes the technologies and tradecraft that enable the mission.

In my professional life since Korea I often reflected on the energy and optimism soldiers had in response to a leader who insisted on taking up the hard challenge of being forward leaning. Over the years I tried to bring a similar approach to my own teams. I've tried to be sure my leaders at all levels were excited and comfortable with constant change, that they could view change as a growth opportunity. I've tried to focus on creating leaders who are confident and capable of planning even on their worst days.

When Accenture released its annual *Technology Vision* report[20] in 2021 our Chief of Technology, Paul Daugherty, observed that COVID effectively hit a fast-forward button, accelerating ten years of change into one or two years. It forced leaders to proactively embrace new ways of connecting with their workforce and their stakeholders. It shoved them into a future defined by new realities.

During the COVID pandemic I paid attention to organizations that may not have predicted the virus but that did have the foresight to ready themselves for crisis. When COVID happened they had the culture and technological foundations they needed. Those who established innovation as a cultural norm, the ones who invested in technologies that enabled collaboration before the crisis, they pivoted quickly. In the face of something unprecedented they found ways to take care of their people, their families, their clients and their communities. They adapted.

Even prepared organizations struggle to pivot in a single step. But leaders whose organizations are accustomed to scanning the horizon for risks and embrace change as a constant had greater success meeting the challenge of changing conditions. The outcome was far less positive for others.

The COVID crisis exposed leaders who found themselves on Day Zero with an organization and a workforce unaccustomed to change and disruption. They were unprepared from a technology, governance and change-management standpoint to reset, to adapt. Many were able to catch up and stabilize. But the experience of failing to be ready for the worst day was costly. I think it was especially painful for teams that struggled for a vision of the way forward while simultaneously sorting their options in the present.

In any age, transformational leaders accept the inevitability of volatility. Leaders who scan the horizon learn to make change work to their advantage. It's possible that COVID may be the catalyst for leaders to think about their relationship to uncertainty. They may learn to think beyond the tyranny of the present.

---

[20] "Leaders Wanted: Masters of Change at a Moment of Truth." *Technology Vision.* Accenture. February 2021.

# Short-Term Execution, Long-Term Vision

## J. Michael Prince

*J. Michael Prince is president and CEO of USPA Global Licensing Inc. (USPAGL), the exclusive worldwide licensor for the United States Polo Association's (USPA), founded in 1890. USPAGL manages the global multibillion-dollar US Polo Assn. brand providing the USPA with a long-term source of revenue that helps support the sport of polo in the United States. US Polo Assn. is a nearly $2 billion sport-inspired lifestyle brand with 1,100 retail stores, an impressive digital presence, and thousands of additional points of sale in 180 countries around the world. In 2020, US Polo Assn. was ranked the fifth largest global sports licensor in the world based on retail sales, with only the National Football League, the National Basketball Association and Major League Baseball being larger.*

*Prince first entered the world of lifestyle brands in 2005 when he became chief financial officer of Converse, the leader among Nike's portfolio of affiliate companies. In 2012 he was a member of the management team that spun off Cole Haan from Nike as its own private entity. From 2013 to 2016 he was president, chief operating officer and board member at Cole Haan.*

*Even before the crisis created by the coronavirus pandemic in 2020, Prince had experience managing and thinking strategically amid uncertainty. Retail had been under intense pressure for at least a decade. When it was further upended by the pandemic in early 2020—supply chains shutting down, stores closing, employees anxious about work—Prince*

152

*drew on his previous experience with crisis: the Great Recession and financial crisis of 2008.*

*The two moments were not the same. But both put a premium on moving fast while still acting thoughtfully. Both taught the lesson of leaders trusting instinct—instinct informed by fact.*

*The essence of prepared leadership is a capacity to make good choices when the present is unfamiliar, and the future is not just unknown but unknowable. In 2020 USPAGL dealt with the crisis immediately with consciously candid communications outreach to staff, global partners and vendors. That built a sense of partnership in engaging the crisis. More than just being the right thing to do it was a long-term strategic bet on the company's future.*

*As time passes it will become harder to remember how abruptly the world shut down in the spring of 2020. The leadership team at USPAGL believed its aggressive response to the situation would lead to new and significant opportunities in a post-crisis world. Prince and his team recognized early on that when crisis ends organizations are long remembered for how they responded.*

*Uncertainty will continue to be a factor in every operating environment in the coming years. It will be a fascinating time to be marketing US Polo Assn.'s classic sport-inspired Americana style around the world. Bonds of trust are tested and need extra attention during inevitable periods of crisis. Leaders who thrive will be distinguished by their flexibility as they pursue strategic ambitions. For all of us, the ways we work—physically together or physically apart—will be affected by safety considerations, technology and the human desire to be together.*

*The experience of USPAGL in 2020 suggests that while much may change the foundation of a brand and its core values can endure.*

There are times when you can draw on the past. In 2008 I was a young CFO for Converse, one of Nike's most profitable global businesses. I remember noticing some negative trends in the marketplace and was feeling concerned that seismic change was coming. We moved quickly and immediately got to work to get in front of what would soon be the 2008 financial crisis and the Great Recession. There were businesses we had worked with that we knew probably weren't going to be around. We started mitigating risks and being more thoughtful about strategies that would protect the business.

Over those very challenging two years the Converse business delivered record results, expanded its global footprint and took market share, which at the time seemed virtually impossible.

Fast-forward to February 2020. I was in a USPAGL board meeting where I had just announced record financial results for the US Polo Assn. brand in 2019 on top of record results for 2018. But on the side I was taking note of a crisis brewing in China and sharing concerns with our board—it was the very beginning of the coronavirus pandemic. At the time all our stores in China had shut down—roughly 100. But I was more concerned about the global supply chain and the impact that could have on our overall business. There was a flashing red light out there, and it didn't look good.

Soon after that meeting many more countries began to shut down and I began using some of my Converse playbook. First, preserve cash flow. We told our vendors we'd make sure they got paid but that we were going to stretch out payments. We told the partners, our licensees, who pay *us* that we were willing to be flexible but that they had to keep steady payments coming to us.

Just three weeks later 90 percent of our stores around the world were closed. Our corporate office was locked down and every employee was working from home. That's how quickly the pandemic hit.

But we got in front of it. There's a balance you need to strike between having experience and understanding the situation you're in. My experience in 2008 helped me develop a playbook for execution. But the other lesson my previous experience gave me was knowing when my gut is telling me I need to pivot, that things have changed. I need to listen to my intuition.

The impact of the pandemic came harder and faster than any of us would have thought. We saw some panic in the very beginning within the ecosystem of relationships we had. But I reminded our strategic partners that we were right there with them during the dark moments. This helped bring about a sense of being in it together as a team. What also helped is the way we communicated and stayed connected. The decisions we made were not just to get us through the moment but to prepare us for the long haul. When I was at Nike we would focus on short-term execution, long-term vision. That's in my DNA now.

There were a couple of times early in the pandemic when I let myself get out over my skies on some things. That feeling, and a couple of early mistakes, helped me slow down, listen and evaluate major decisions more thoughtfully, all while remaining on the offense.

One of the decisions we made early on, for example, was that no matter how challenging things became we were going to stay positive and factual, always giving people a reason to keep pushing forward.

The communications piece was central. Almost every week we sent out messaging to staff and partners around the world to assure them we were all in this together. We made sure the leadership team was communicating with *their* teams routinely and that the people reporting to them were communicating with *their* teams. We shared that it was going to be tough. We told them the business would take a short-term hit. But if we worked through it together and managed through the coming months the future had significant promise. That's how we looked at it.

Getting people to follow you is hard when they're afraid and uncertain. No matter how bad it gets you've got to make sure people trust you. Something I noticed during the crisis was that many well-respected companies suddenly broke the level of trust with their employees. When the trust level is gone it makes it hard for folks to come back and stay motivated.

Because we were truthful from the start the trust was there. When we said we were going to make it safe to come back to the office people believed that was the case. And when they did come back in we proved it.

In 2020 we reopened our headquarters in early June as the state of Florida reopened. Some people were a little hesitant about returning, and that was understandable. We started with a skeleton crew with everyone wearing face covers. We installed hand sanitizer stations, scheduled our cleaning crew to regularly sanitize workstations, implemented rotating schedules and enforced social distancing. The next week we brought in a few more people in staggered shifts. As people came back they reengaged. They were excited to be in a new environment and to see their colleagues. And they were reassured by the safety precautions we put in place.

I'm a Gen Xer. I'm someone who likes the structure of an office and I like being able to come in every day. But what I learned is that I don't have to be in the office five days a week to get things done. Maybe I'll be in the office three days a week and have flex schedules for our employees long-term. We will see and continue to pivot.

I also think the way we travel for business will be very different going forward. Before the pandemic I traveled a lot. I liked it, and I liked seeing the person I was talking to, negotiating with, strategizing with. But I've realized I don't need to travel as much to get things done or to be successful.

When I think about the future I know some of the traditional ways people work should always be there. But adaptability, flexibility, the use of technology in the right ways—all that, it just accelerated during the pandemic. The way people work is changed forever. If they don't adapt there will be a lot of executives who get lost in the tailwind.

As the official brand of the USPA, US Polo Assn. is truly sport-inspired, which cuts through a lot of clutter in the retail space. There's also something about the connection to both the sport and horse culture—perhaps the beauty and excitement—that seems to resonate around the world.

Global consumers embrace classic Americana more than most people realize. And US Polo Assn. is one of the most democratic brands in the world—anyone can wear it, look good, and have a piece of the sport. I'm generalizing here but the point is, it's a brand that is truly democratic and universal.

US Polo Assn. is sold in 180 countries—more than 90 percent of the world. We sell a sport-inspired lifestyle that we're never going to depart from though it may evolve. Millennials and Gen Z consumers especially respond to what we represent. The world is just so much more connected than it was 20 years ago, which is a great thing for all of us. While we are coming through a period of great challenge I also believe in the human spirit and our ability to adapt, innovate and embrace a brighter future.

# Author Bios

## L. Kevin Kelly

Kevin Kelly was raised in Virginia and received a Bachelor of Science from George Mason University and an MBA from Duke University, for which he later served on the Board of Advisors for the Fuqua School of Business. Kelly has lived and worked all over the world, including Tokyo, London, New York and Chicago.

Kelly began what would become his pivotal role in leadership consultancy at the executive search firm, Heidrick & Struggles. As chief executive of Heidrick & Struggles, Kelly transformed an already successful company into a modern global leadership-consulting firm operating in 60 countries.

Kelly joined the Heidrick & Struggles' Tokyo office in 1997. He later served as regional managing partner of Asia Pacific and then Europe, the Middle East, and Africa from 2001 to 2006. He became chief executive officer in 2006.

Throughout his career, Kelly has focused on the challenges of leadership and has authored three books on the subject: *CEO: The Low Down on the Top Job* (2008), *Top Jobs: How They Are Different and What You Need to Succeed* (2009), and *Leading in Turbulent Times* (2010).

Kelly's expertise played a pivotal role in defining the new terms of engagement between technology and talent in the early 2000s with creative joint ventures encompassing NASDAQ and the Economist Intelligence Unit. He also collaborated with the World Economic Forum's Young Global Leaders program, contributing to the community's personal development as contemporary leaders.

After Heidrick & Struggles, Kelly became the president and CEO of Asia Pulp and Paper NA. In that role, Kelly deepened his understanding of doing business in China and across Southeast Asia. By building trusted relationships and advocating for high standards of transparency, Kelly was able to maintain the integrity of the business's supply chains and introduce world-class sustainability standards.

Today, as CEO of Halo Privacy, Kelly has transitioned to a privacy activist, working to ensure individual protections in an increasingly more threatening digital landscape. He also continues his leadership consultancy with both *Fortune* 500 companies and various trade groups, ensuring that the fostering of talented individuals continues to evolve in an ever-changing global marketplace.

## Lieutenant General John F. Mulholland Jr. (Retired)

The proud son of a USAF fighter pilot and Korean War veteran, Lieutenant General Mulholland John F. Mulholland, Jr. (Retired) was born in Clovis, New Mexico, and grew up in Bethesda, Maryland. He earned a Bachelor of Arts in History and was commissioned as a Second Lieutenant of Infantry, United States Army, upon graduating from Furman University.

As a young infantry officer Mulholland served as platoon leader of both mechanized and airborne rifle platoons, as well as a mortar platoon leader. After joining the 1st Special Forces Regiment in 1983 Mulholland commanded from the captain through lieutenant general-level in Army and in joint special-operations forces. He served as Deputy Commanding General, Joint Special Operations Command, as the Commanding General, United States Army Special Operations Command, and as the 15th Deputy Commander, United States Special Operations Command.

Following graduation from the National War College in 2001, then—Col. Mulholland assumed command of the 5th Special Forces Group, Airborne, at Fort Campbell, Kentucky. In the immediate aftermath of the 9/11 attacks on the United States, Colonel Mulholland commanded Joint Special Operations Task Force-North

(Task Force Dagger) in the opening days of Operation Enduring Freedom and, later, Combined Joint Special Operations Task Force-West in the initial campaign of Operation Iraqi Freedom.

Mulholland's overseas assignments included two tours in the former Panama Canal Zone; command of the 1$^{st}$ Battalion, 1$^{st}$ Special Forces Group, Okinawa; and Chief, Office of Military Cooperation, Kuwait. Mulholland completed his final tour on active duty as the Associate Director of Military Affairs, Central Intelligence Agency.

Mulholland currently resides in Alexandria, Virginia, with his wife, the former Miriam Mitchell, and his partner in Mulholland Consulting LLC.

## Kevin McDermott

Kevin McDermott is the founder of Collective Intelligence and a principal in the well-known scenario-planning firm, Futures Strategy Group.

Working in countries around the world, McDermott has served an international client portfolio that includes General Motors, IBM, Innosight, A.T. Kearney, Korn-Ferry, MasterCard Advisors, McKinsey & Co., Robert Wood Johnson Foundation, Spencer Stuart, United Way of America and financial services startups.

McDermott spent the early part of his career as an award-winning reporter and editor covering international trade and economics. His international bylines included reporting from France for the *Washington Post* and *Saveur*, from the United Kingdom for the *New York Times*, and from Haiti for the *Atlantic Monthly.*

McDermott lives in New York with his wife and two children.

www.ingramcontent.com/pod-product-compliance
Lightning Source LLC
Chambersburg PA
CBHW021414210526
45463CB00001B/364